The Ano

# The

# 24

problems, barrenness,
famines and turning it
around

The sudden
breakthroughs of God

# Hour
# Miracle

Volume Two

# Matthew Ashimolowo

© 2002 Matthew Ashimolowo

Published by Mattyson Media an imprint of
MAMM
Matthew Ashimolowo Media Ministries
57 Waterden Road
Hackney Wick
London
E15 2EE

ISBN: 1-874-646-538

Bible quotes are from the King James version
Bible
unless otherwise stated.

# CONTENTS

Introduction........................................................ 5

**Chapter 1**
    **ISRAEL** (Breaking the Power of
        Prolonged Bondage)............................ **9**
    The Battle Before the Breakthrough............. 14
    The Midnight Before the Miracle.................. 21
    The Sudden Attack Before the 24 Hour
        Miracle.................................................. 28
    The 24 Hour Miracle..................................... 32

**Chapter 2**
    **THE FOUR LEPERS** (From the
        Rejected to the Selected)..................... **41**
    The Problem Before the 24 Hour Miracle.... 45
    The Process For the 24 Hour Miracle........... 50
    Entering the 24 Hour Miracle....................... 57

**Chapter 3**
    **MORDECAI** (From Bondage to
        Breakthrough).................................... **69**
    The Problems Before the Breakthrough........ 76
    The Process................................................... 81
    The 24 Hour Miracle..................................... 95

Chapter 4

# MEPHIBOSETH (From Rejection to

Restoration)...................................... **111**

The Catalogue of Troubles.............................. 114

The Call From the Palace................................ 124

The 24 Hour Miracle...................................... 128


**Testimonies**........................................................ **141**

# INTRODUCTION

I love taking flights to various destinations; I love the sights of airports, particularly the busy ones; the Heathrows, Gatwicks, Charles de Gaulles and JFKs of this world. But imagine getting to the airport, checking in and taking your seat in the plane. All other passengers too are ready, everyone seated in their place.

The "fasten your seatbelt" sign is already on, the plane has even taxied, but then suddenly it is held in a hold pattern. There are other planes in front of you; the pilot comes on the public address system on the plane to announce that because of busyness, passenger lateness and the need to off load some baggage, your flight is now on hold. The plane is full of fuel but you cannot go, because you are now in a hold pattern.

Life sometimes feels that way, you want to make progress, and you feel you are ready but you cannot quite make the move, something seems to keep you in the hold pattern.

Single? Yes, of the appropriate age, but it does not seem to happen. Educated? Yes, you have read all you can, but it is so hard to get the job that agrees with your qualification. Ministry? Yes, you have prayed, fasted and done all they said to do to get a successful ministry, but your realities do not seem to match the efforts invested.

You are waiting to occupy a house of your own but it is taking so long. Some matters in life even take longe; it seems as if you never graduate to the things you are meant to do.

Wait a minute, suddenly it is probably an announcement or a letter through your pigeon hole, a phone call, someone visiting abruptly, a message on your voicemail asking that you return the call, a very supernatural spiritual encounter, at least that is how you can describe it because it is out of the ordinary and it suddenly swings things around. Things begin to change so fast in a short time that your movement forward is almost faster than that of light (310,000 kilometres per second).

We are not alone in this experience; the Scripture will say of the saints of old:

Now all these things happened unto them for ensamples: and they are written for our admonition, upon whom the ends of the world are come.
1 Corinthians 10:11 (KJV)

God recently opened my eyes to see the anointing of the 24 hour miracle, how that you could go on in a challenging situation for long, but then suddenly God is able to burst upon your situation and advance you further than you can imagine in a short time.

> For his anger endureth but a moment; in his favour is life: weeping may endure for a night, but joy cometh in the morning.
> Psalms 30:5 (KJV)

The night seasons of life often look unending and as if we would not survive, but the Scriptures give us an insight and that is the fact that all night seasons have a limited time span.

I want to present to you cases of God intervening and in a short time; the space of 24 hours, taking the problem that had gone on for a long time and swinging it around.

# CHAPTER 1

# ISRAEL

## Breaking the power of prolonged bondage

We have established that in all of God's deliverances where the 24 hour miracle takes place, God allows his people to go through a process. For some it is an intense rejection by other people. For others it is a midnight hour that seems to last for ever. For Israel it was being in perpetual slavery for 430 years. At such times there are so many questions for which there is no answer. At such times we ask, "Why God why, when God when, how God how, who God who?" The questions are almost endless for which there is many times no answer. If God must answer, all the purpose of the process would be aborted. You will have to go through that valley of the shadow of death.

Israel's slavery went on as if there was no end and when it was time for them to be released, Pharaoh would not let go. He made no room for the day when Jehovah would come for His firstborn Son. Every plague sent met with

Pharaoh's defiance, until the final plague; the death of Egypt's first-born for tampering with God's first-born, Israel.

That was a turning point for Pharaoh to decide it was time to yield; that was also a turning point for Israel to experience the anointing of the 24 hour miracle. It was that moment when all the death that took place was in the camp of Egypt and not of Israel as previously it had been. The tables had turned around; the wailing was now in the camp of Egypt. All the crying which was in Goshen had been replaced by a voice of celebration. All the sadness and bereavement in Goshen had changed, now the tables had turned. The sound of wailing was only in the camp of the enemy. When a people's season for a 24 hour miracle comes, demons tremble; they begin to shake because their time is limited and the season of victory has come for the people of God.

When God ushers you into the season of the 24 hour miracle, you may not see it with your natural eyes, but in the realm of the Spirit you are mighty through God to the pulling down of strongholds.

(For the weapons of our warfare are not carnal, but mighty through God to the pulling down of strong holds;)
2 Corinthians 10:4 (KJV)

The alarm has gone off in satan's domain. The sound in the ear of every demon is the fact that their time is up and they are about to be sent packing. It is not how long the demon has held you down or fought you; when God's invasion begins, it must still let go of you.

It is not how long sickness has fought you; when Jehovah Rapha steps in, your healing will be established.

And said, If thou wilt diligently hearken to the voice of
the LORD thy God, and wilt do that which is right in
his sight, and wilt give ear to his commandments, and
keep all his statutes, I will put none of these diseases
upon thee, which I have brought upon the Egyptians:
for I am the LORD that healeth thee.
Exodus 15:26 (KJV)

There is already a sign in the Spirit realm; you can hear the voice of the Holy Spirit when the time has come for the immigration of God's people. It is time to resist the devil and he will let you go. Hear what James said.

Submit yourselves therefore to God. Resist the devil,
and he will flee from you.
James 4:7 (KJV)

It is a new day and the enemy is running scared.

Satan cannot stand it when an army arises in the earth that is militant and knows its right. He cannot stand it when we become aggressive and go after what belongs to us. Satan cannot handle it when a people rise who have made up their minds to claim their rights and full possession. It gives him a headache, it causes him diarrhoea. He tries to tighten the noose, but it is too late for the devil. Our victory is assured if we understand the mantle we carry; the mantle of the 24 hour miracle.

And the children of Israel went away, and did as the LORD had commanded Moses and Aaron, so did they. And it came to pass, that at midnight the LORD smote all the firstborn in the land of Egypt, from the firstborn of Pharaoh that sat on his throne unto the firstborn of the captive that was in the dungeon; and all the firstborn of cattle. And Pharaoh rose up in the night, he, and all his servants, and all the Egyptians; and there was a great cry in Egypt; for there was not a house where there was not one dead. And he called for Moses and Aaron by night, and said, Rise up, and get you forth from among my people, both ye and the children of Israel; and go, serve the LORD, as ye have said. Also take your flocks and your herds, as ye have said, and be gone; and bless me also. And the Egyptians were urgent upon the people, that they might send them out of the land in haste; for they said, We be all dead men. And the people took their dough before it was leavened, their kneadingtroughs being bound up in their clothes upon their shoulders. And the children of Israel did according to the word of Moses; and they borrowed of the Egyptians jewels of silver, and jewels of gold, and raiment: And the LORD gave the people favour in the sight of the Egyptians, so that they lent unto them such things as they required. And they spoiled the Egyptians.

Exodus 12:28-36 (KJV)

# THE BATTLE BEFORE THE BREAKTHROUGH

We have already stated the fact that battles always precede the 24 hour miracle. God makes His promise to us and makes us go through the process that gets us ready for the blessing.

The story of Israel which we consider in this chapter, may not directly state everything about the process, but it is obvious that prior to their 24 hour miracle they went through:

## 1. Being generational doormats

Deprived of every benefit, right and thing that would advance their place in life, they were then treated as doormats. They had a habit of withdrawing what would help people, their economic, financial and social emancipation, in the attempt to keep them perpetually subservient. The apartheid of South Africa, I am told, only encouraged blacks in courses particularly that have to do with teacher training and other middle level professions. They were rarely encouraged to train as engineers or medical doctors.

Israel did not have enough education. As slaves they did not have any money, they did not have any time of their own. Their slave-masters allotted whatever time they had to them. Children born in this circumstance certainly wouldgo through intense, bad childhood experiences. Israel was used and abused by their masters. Not long after a person was born in Egypt in those days, it becomes obvious to them if they were born on the right or wrong side of town. Goshen certainly spelt trouble. Just being born in the area where you were regarded as a doormat. The family was seen as wrong and the timing; being born in the days of slavery, for one to have the right to choose when to come to the world, was like being the worst season to manifest.

It certainly must have made them to regret being born at all. Probably one of the great contradictions was to be called Israel and yet be in slavery. A prince of God held by the princes of men. Sometimes an enemy will try to use the environment to define who we are. The devil likes it when we are ignorant of who we are.

My people are destroyed for lack of knowledge: because thou hast rejected knowledge, I will also reject thee, that thou shalt be no priest to me: seeing thou hast forgotten the law of thy God, I will also forget thy children.
Hosea 4:6 (KJV)

## 2. They went through generational delays

Not only were they treated as doormats for generations they also found that they had to go through intense delay for their emancipation. Sometimes we believe God for a quick change in the area of our finances, restoration of all our stolen property, a godly partner, promotion at work, an advancement on our job, uncommon favour upon our business and it seems like it just would not come forever and we are tempted to give up.

It does not matter how long it takes, it is always too soon to give up. After all you are not the first to experience a delay. Paul encourages that having done everything you know to do, the next best thing to do is to stand.

> Finally, my brethren, be strong in the Lord, and in the
> power of his might.
> Ephesians 6:10 (KJV)

A delay is a challenging experience; it leaves one with a lot of questions. "When will it happen?" "Why is there a delay?" "What did I do wrong?" "What else did I need to do?"

When you look closely at delays, there seems to be 3 people in the picture.

# 1.    God

Because He has better plans:

Now when they had gone throughout Phrygia and the
region of Galatia, and were forbidden of the Holy
Ghost to preach the word in Asia,
After they were come to Mysia, they assayed to go into
Bithynia: but the Spirit suffered them not.
Acts 16:6-7 (KJV)

Some things seem obvious and good because they seem
to agree with other good things.  It seems obvious and
good that Paul should go to the region where he wanted
to go and preach.  After all the Great Commission says,
to "Go".  Yet we answer ultimately to the sovereign God.
In His sovereignty and Omniscience He knows the
master plan and we must wait for His command.
If you go where you want to go and miss
where God wants you to go, you will be out
of your assignment and out of your divine appointment.

And a vision appeared to Paul in the night; There stood
a man of Macedonia, and prayed him, saying, Come
over into Macedonia, and help us.  And after he had
seen the vision, immediately we endeavoured to go into
Macedonia, assuredly gathering that the Lord had called
us for to preach the gospel unto them.
Acts 16:9-10 (KJV)

When God stands between your plan and gives an instruction that either says no or wait a while, it must mean that He has a better time, place, method and subsequently a greater breakthrough which can only come in the time of His choosing.

## 2.    Satan can cause delay.

But we, brethren, being taken from you for a short time in presence, not in heart, endeavoured the more abundantly to see your face with great desire.
Wherefore we would have come unto you, even I Paul, once and again; but Satan hindered us.
1 Thessalonians 2:17-18 (KJV)

Satan's purpose in causing a delay is to abort destinies, frustrate people's faith. It is to cause a delay and make people doubt the goodness of God. Yet satan's hold can only be for a short while because the 24 hour miracle anointing will burst upon satan's delay and you will be held down no more.

## 3.    You can be the cause of your own delay

When Israel left Egypt and travelled in the wilderness, it was kept in the hold and refused the benefit of entering Canaan because of its own disobedience, because of its walk in unbelief.

Delay could come because one is not sowing

the appropriate seed that will cause a harvest to come. Delays will come because you are sowing seed or doing significant things with very little effort.

> Ye have sown much, and bring in little; ye eat, but ye have not enough; ye drink, but ye are not filled with drink; ye clothe you, but there is none warm; and he that earneth wages earneth wages to put it into a bag with holes. Thus saith the LORD of hosts; Consider your ways.
>
> Haggai 1:6-7 (KJV)

So when your zeal, your inspiration and hope wanes. when your 'go get it' attitude towards the things of God is replaced with a nonchalant attitude, delays follow. Delays result in:

**i.    Disinterest**

> Hope deferred maketh the heart sick: but when the desire cometh, it is a tree of life.
>
> Proverbs 13:12 (KJV)

You cannot be passive about the things which you were passionate and not find yourself delayed from receiving the blessing you ought to receive. Passive people do not receive surpassing blessing. When you lose interest in what God says you become unfruitful because you are not hearing God.

## ii.    Discouragement

Discouraged because the promise has been delayed.

> For the vision is yet for an appointed time, but at the
> end it shall speak, and not lie: though it tarry, wait for it;
> because it will surely come, it will not tarry.
> Habbakuk 2:3 (KJV)

In our estimation the promise has been delayed, because while on one hand we know and understand that all we need is to walk with God by faith and not put a time limit on Him, yet our finite mind will often be discouraged and when things do not happen at the time we thought it should.   We become disenfranchised.  If God were to answer our prayers at the times we choose, we would have found out that we had asked for some doors to open five years, ten years too early.

## iii.    Dissatisfaction

People who have been in the hold because they have held on waiting for the fulfilment of a promise and the time they think it should happen has come and gone, could easily become dissatisfied.

# THE MIDNIGHT BEFORE THE MIRACLE

What does a believer do in the midnight hour? What is the midnight hour anyway? Midnight in scripture is often the evening time when challenges come and there is little help. The Bible will often use the midnight hour, that is the season we go through things without enough help. Jacob wrestled with the angel at midnight. Paul and Silas were alone in the prison when they sang at midnight. At midnight, the four lepers walked towards the camp of the Syrians, not knowing what their faith was. Jesus' parable talked of the enemy who sowed seed at midnight. Most of the first born of Egypt died at midnight.

Christians do go through midnight hours, but how should they carry themselves, because how you behave in your midnight hour determines your strength at the breaking of day.

But they that wait upon the LORD shall renew their strength; they shall mount up with wings as eagles; they shall run, and not be weary; and they shall walk, and not faint.
Isaiah 40:31 (KJV)

A strong characteristic of those who are able to over-come the midnight malady is the ability to wait, yet society no longer wants to wait. We are the impatient generation, an attitude that has no room for waiting. We are the computerised society, the push button mentality people. We are the "do it now", "do it quick", "do it fast" generation and this mentality has been imported into Christianity. We have not recognised the fine line between the walk of faith and the selfish desire for things to happen quick, even if they are outside the purpose and counsel of God.

God on the other hand will not degenerate to become a push button sovereign. He reigns in the affairs of men. We must learn the ability to wait and in our waiting we must do what His Word says. His Word says, "Having done all to stand".

## 1.    Having done all to stand

Wherefore take unto you the whole armour of God,
that ye may be able to withstand in the evil day, and
having done all, to stand.
Ephesians 6:13 (KJV)

"Having done all to stand" means you have a checklist of the things to do and you have done all you need to do and now you are waiting for His move. You have done all the financials, you have done all you need for the healing, you have done all you need for the deliverances, you have done all you need for the move of God, you have done all you need for the salvation of loved ones, you have done all you need for your own breakthrough, you have done all you need for the testimony. "Having done all to stand".

This is the first thing you do at midnight.

## 2.  Develop an expectant heart

Expectation births manifestation. You cannot have manifested blessing in a place where there is no expectation. It is important to keep on waiting to receive until the breakthrough comes.

Do not say, I will repay evil; wait [expectantly] for the
Lord, and He will rescue you
(Proverbs 20:22 - Amp)

For the vision is yet for an appointed time and it hastens to the end [fulfillment]; it will not deceive or disappoint.
Though it tarry, wait [earnestly] for it, because it will surely come; it will not be behind hand on its appointed
day.
[Habbakuk 2:3 -Amp]

## 3.  Be not offended at God

How finite the human mind is, it easily forgets all of the goodness of God.

How precious also are thy thoughts unto me, O God!
how great is the sum of them!
Psalms 139:17 (KJV)

But God, who is rich in mercy, for his great love where-
with he loved us,
Ephesians 2:4 (KJV)

It overlooks the summary of God's love; it tends to focus on what has not happened. The healing yet to be which is yet to manifest. In that state of mind people take offence at God.

The year was 1978, I had left Bible School in 1976 and was an assistant pastor at Foursquare Gospel Church, Shomolu, Lagos, Nigeria. For some reason in March of 78 I began to plan to go to study for a degree in Theology at the parent bible college of the one I had attended, this time in Los Angeles. Every effort made met with frustration. I was six years old in the Lord, four years old in ministry and naive about the things of God. I took every obstacle to mean satan was hindering me. Though I had trepidations in my spirit I did not understand that it could mean that this delay was because the total plan of my study was not commanded of the Lord.

I forced myself until I had to travel. Firstly I had to stop in Amsterdam and reapply at the American Embassy and was told they had to hear from Nigeria. The School gave me the go ahead to travel over to the United States, since it had already made arrangements with Los Angeles Airport officials for my visa to be issued on arrival. However, my first point of entry into the US was Chicago and the immigration staff were not satisfied with my arrival at Chicago wihout a visa.

American immigration advised that I withdraw my application or may not be able to enter the United States any more. I had left home for 12 days now, I had given away all my belongings. I had been sent off properly by the local church where I had been assistant pastor. What do I go back to? The embarrassment, the pain, the shame. With nowhere else to go I summoned courage to go back to the place where I was celebrated anyway. On the flight from Chicago to Amsterdam from where I would catch my flight to Lagos, I went through intense pain and began to take offence at God. The drama of it all was while I was offended at God and would not want Him to speak to me, I was also witnessing to the person seated next to me.

With hindsight today it was obvious that were I to have settled in America and studied Christian education which I had initially gone for, I would have been a specialist at opening Sunday Schools and have missed whatever was in God's ultimate plan for me.

## 4.    Make a decision

Movement in any direction starts with a decision and since you are getting ready for a 24 hour miracle, you must make the decision that will help you.  Make a decision not to go with the flow of whatever one is doing outside of the will of God; make a decision to glorify God with your life. Make a decision not to allow yourself to join any negative conversation.

The grass withereth, the flower fadeth: but the word of our God shall stand for ever.
Isaiah 40:8 (KJV)

Make a decision that irrespective of how you feel you know that God cannot lie and therefore you will depend upon His Word.

For I know the thoughts that I think toward you, saith the LORD, thoughts of peace, and not of evil, to give you an expected end.
Jeremiah 29:11 (KJV)

So shall my word be that goeth forth out of my mouth: it shall not return unto me void, but it shall accomplish that which I please, and it shall prosper in the thing whereto I sent it.
Isaiah 55:11 (KJV)

The words of the LORD are pure words: as silver tried
in a furnace of earth, purified seven times.
Psalms 12:6 (KJV)

Make a decision to think differently to how everyone else
thinks.

I beseech you therefore, brethren, by the mercies of
God, that ye present your bodies a living sacrifice, holy,
acceptable unto God, which is your reasonable service.
And be not conformed to this world: but be ye trans-
formed by the renewing of your mind, that ye may
prove what is that good, and acceptable, and perfect,
will of God.
Romans 12:1-2 (KJV)

A godly thought pattern is what reflects the mind of
Christ in you.

Let this mind be in you, which was also in Christ Jesus:
Philippians 2:5 (KJV)

# THE SUDDEN ATTACK BEFORE THE 24 HOUR MIRACLE

And the same day, when the even was come, he saith
unto them, Let us pass over unto the other side.
And when they had sent away the multitude, they took
him even as he was in the ship. And there were also
with him other little ships. And there arose a great
storm of wind, and the waves beat into the ship, so that
it was now full.
Mark 4:35-37 (KJV)

The story is clear, Jesus had instructed His disciples; they were crossing the Galilean Sea to the other side. When the journey began there was no cloud in the sky, but suddenly there was a great storm. Satan had an unexpected storm to try to frustrate the programme Jesus had. A furious storm of hurricane proportions had suddenly risen. You are engaged in the mode for a miracle, God is about to break forth upon your life. The enemy knows that once he lets you go, once you gain your freedom, he cannot hold you back, so he will throw everything he has in the attempt to frustrate the 24 hour miracle.

People who do not see your vision, people who like you the way you have always been. If you would just get discouraged and give up your dream. A spouse who does not realise they are about to hinder the best thing that will happen to you. A friend who does not realise that friendship with them is taking away the values you have always held.

Whatever storm made Peter, James and John afraid must have been ferocious. These are men who were raised by the Galilean Sea, whose life wove around fishing and therefore must have been very well accustomed to the storms around the Sea. This is exactly what satan wanted, a bunch of discouraged, fearful and timid followers of Jesus. Fear has torment, fear steals your blessing, it stops the wave of breakthrough, but Jesus arose and rebuked the storm.

And he arose, and rebuked the wind, and said unto the sea, Peace, be still. And the wind ceased, and there was a great calm.
Mark 4:39 (KJV)

Mark Chapter 4:37 tells us what kind of a storm it was. A great storm of wind. Verse 39 tells us what kind of calm there was when Jesus rebuked the storm. A great calm. The Greek word for great here is 'Megas'. The same word which described the suddenness of the storm - 'sudden mega storm' - shows us that Jesus arose to bring the storm to a stop.

A 'mega' calm came. So the Scripture is saying you will go from a mega storm to a mega calm, from mega nothing to mega abundance, from mega attack to mega victory, from mega empty net to mega net breaking breakthrough. You have been giving and tithing, suddenly mega abundance. In effect whatever mega negative is going on now, get ready for a mega positive, get ready for a mega result.

The greatness of the problem will be met with the greatness of God. The word 'megas' means:

§   Abundant
§   Completely
§   Fearlessly
§   Greatly
§   Greater
§   Greater things
§   All more
§   Huge
§   Large
§   Larger
§   Mighty
§   Strongly
§   Terribly
§   Surprisingly

Whatever it is and whatever way it comes, you should get ready for a mega response from our God. No matter how intense the battle is, it will meet with a mega God who has a mega response to whatever tries to touch His children.

Ye are of God, little children, and have overcome them: because greater is he that is in you, than he that is in the world.
1 John 4:4 (KJV)

Cast not away therefore your confidence, which hath great recompence of reward.
Hebrews 10:35 (KJV)

# Be 'mega' minded as you wait on God.

Wait for a mega restoration, wait for God to step in and turn the battle that has gone on for so long.

# THE 24 HOUR MIRACLE

The mega God has arrived on the scenario, suddenly every chain that had held the people of God for 430 years was about to experience His mega power. The people who cried to God for a long time suddenly found that the answer came. The people who sat in darkness have seen a great light.

The people which sat in darkness saw great light; and to them which sat in the region and shadow of death light is sprung up.
Matthew 4:16 (KJV)

Suddenly out of darkness merges:

## 1.    Mega-physical freedom

And he called for Moses and Aaron by night, and said, Rise up, and get you forth from among my people, both ye and the children of Israel; and go, serve the LORD, as ye have said.
Exodus 12:31 (KJV)

If God be for you, no ailment, sickness or disease, pain - physical or emotional will be

# able to stop you.

The mega God promises to deliver and set you free. Physical healing is the bona-fide favour and blessing of God's people. So may you experience it in a mega-way.

And said, If thou wilt diligently hearken to the voice of the LORD thy God, and wilt do that which is right in his sight, and wilt give ear to his commandments, and keep all his statutes, I will put none of these diseases upon thee, which I have brought upon the Egyptians: for I am the LORD that healeth thee.
Exodus 15:26 (KJV)

And ye shall serve the LORD your God, and he shall bless thy bread, and thy water; and I will take sickness away from the midst of thee.
There shall nothing cast their young, nor be barren, in thy land: the number of thy days I will fulfil.
Exodus 23:25-26 (KJV)

That it might be fulfilled which was spoken by Esaias the prophet, saying, Himself took our infirmities, and bare our sicknesses.
Matthew 8:17 (KJV)

Surely he hath borne our griefs, and carried our sorrows: yet we did esteem him stricken, smitten of God, and afflicted. But he was wounded for our transgressions, he was bruised for our iniquities: the chastisement of our peace was upon him; and with his stripes we are healed. All we like sheep have gone astray; we have turned every one to his own way; and the LORD hath laid on him the iniquity of us all. He was oppressed, and he was afflicted, yet he opened not his mouth: he is brought as a lamb to the slaughter, and as a sheep before her shearers is dumb, so he openeth not his mouth.

Isaiah 53:4-7 (KJV)

Within 24 hours they had mega freedom to worship God.

And he called for Moses and Aaron by night, and said, Rise up, and get you forth from among my people, both ye and the children of Israel; and go, serve the LORD, as ye have said.

Exodus 12:31 (KJV)

Egypt was a land of idols; they had a god for everything. The 10 plagues which God brought was to humble the 10 great gods of Egypt.

**Blood** was to humble **'Hapi'**
**Frogs** were to humble **'Heqt'** - This was considered the goddess who was connected to the fertility of the land.
**Lice** were to humble **'Hathor'**
**Flies** were to humble **' Shu'** or **'Isis'**
**Livestock diseased** was to humble **'Apis'**
**Boils** were to humble **'Seqhmat'**
**Hail** was to humilitate **'Geb'**

**Locusts** were to humiliate **'Serapis'**
**Darkness** was to humiliate **'Rah'** - Rah was believed to be the sun god who provided warmth and sunshine from day to day  The darkness therefore challenged the faithfullness of this their sun god
The **killing of the first born** was to humble Pharaoh who believed he was a descendant of the gods

Yet our God will not share His glory with anyone.  He was known to Egypt on this night with the 24 hour break-through as the God who must be worshipped.

## 2.    Mega restoration of their businesses

Also take your flocks and your herds, as ye have said,
and be gone; and bless me also.
Exodus 12:32 (KJV)

Suddenly we read of slaves who owned nothing, now the Egyptians had asked that they take their flocks and herds. God had suddenly put in their hand restoration of their business.  It is not hard for God to take you from nothing to abundance when you are under the influence of the 24 hour miracle.  Things will begin to break forth for you beyond your imagination.

## 3.    Mega favour

... Rise up, and get you forth from among my
people, both ye and the children of Israel; and go, serve
the LORD, as ye have said.
Exodus 12:31 (KJV)

The One who held them down, now gives them uncommon freedom, freedom to move on. Every certificate of slavery was struck off in one moment. The people now were free again; free to serve the Lord to be who God called them to be.

## 4. Restoration of the rights to become a blessing to the nation

> ... and bless me also.
> Exodus 12:32 (KJV)

The one who held them in bondage now seeks the prayer of these ex-slaves, because greater is He that is in you.

> Ye are of God, little children, and have overcome them: because greater is he that is in you, than he that is in the world.
> 1 John 4:4 (KJV)

There is more to you than meets the eye. Do not let a problem define your person. Do not take your identity from the trouble you go through. The most painful thing in Scriptures are the people in the New Testament who were described by their problems. The woman with the issue of blood, the man who was born blind, the lame man by the Beautiful Gate. These people seem to have no name, no fixed address, they took their identity from their challenges. If you have done so hitherto, under the influence of a 24 hour miracle, God will shatter the grip of every problem that gave you a name.

# 5.    Mega restoration of rags to riches

And the people took their dough before it was leavened, their kneadingtroughs being bound up in their
clothes upon their shoulders.
And the children of Israel did according to the word of
Moses; and they borrowed of the Egyptians jewels of
silver, and jewels of gold, and raiment:
Exodus 12:34-35 (KJV)

There is something about the 24 hour anointing. It
seemed to take along a massive prosperity wherever it
goes. God caused Israel to plunder the Egyptians for
their 430 years which their forefathers serve and they
served. They collected the back-pay in one day. They
walked out of the enemy's camp blessed, not broke. God
stopped the day of barely getting by.

Some times Christians go through trouble and come out
surviving. It is not enough to survive, it is important to
come out with a testimony. It may be great to sing the
song "How I got over, my soul looks back in wonder",
but it is important to not only get over it but to come out
of it with a testimony and a promotion.

Israel carried out everything that should have been theirs
in the first place. God got it back for them in a mega way.
Every stolen property must be restored.

When a 24 hour anointing comes upon your life you are like a sheriff with a warrant of arrest on the enemy and a warrant to dispossess him of all stolen property.

It is time for the believer reading this passage to look the devil eyeball to eyeball and boldly proclaim, "I want my stuff back".

Every wealth laid aside by the sinner was restored to them in a mega way. In the days of your restoration you will have much more than what you lost. Get ready for mega improvement, mega increase, mega multiplication. Yes, everything satan stole has to be restored back seven-fold.

Men do not despise a thief, if he steal to satisfy his soul when he is hungry; But if he be found, he shall restore sevenfold; he shall give all the substance of his house.
Proverbs 6:30-31 (KJV)

## 6. They received mega favours, the Egyptians looked favourably on the Israelites.

They received whatever they asked for. In the days of the 24 hour anointing God says call on me, and I will show you and I will give you.

Call unto me, and I will answer thee, and shew thee great and mighty things, which thou knowest not.
Jeremiah 33:3 (KJV)

Ask of me, and I shall give thee the heathen for thine inheritance, and the uttermost parts of the earth for thy possession.

Psalms 2:8 (KJV)

For 430 years Israel struggled under the bondage of the slave master. It seemed like it would not end. Every generation was hopeful, unknown to them that the days had been fixed and it was only known to the omniscient God. When finally the fullness of time had come, within 24 hours, a process of restoration began. Restored back to glory, restored back to blessing. Their days of slavery were turned to a stepping-stone to greater things.

In 24 hours God broke satan's back. Within 24 hours every 'stuff' he had stolen was taken back from him. After all it never belonged to him anyway.

Men do not despise a thief, if he steal to satisfy his soul when he is hungry; But if he be found, he shall restore sevenfold; he shall give all the substance of his house.

Proverbs 6:30-31 (KJV)

God broke down satan's bank and took everything there, handing it over to His people. Restoration in God's programme means to become better, improved, increased and multiplied; all in 24 hours.

# CHAPTER 2

# THE FOUR LEPERS

## From the rejected to the selected

The interesting thing about life is when people feel they have been rejected, they sometimes make no effort to change their image. When people have been classified, they accept other people's definition of who they are.

They fail to realise that if you can be classified, you can also be nullified and if you allow situations, circumstances, situational ethics, the troubles you are going through to define you or compartmentalise you, you become known for a certain problem and are described by it.

For example, the woman with the issue of blood, the man who was born blind, the paralytic man. These are people who took their identity from the problems they were confronted with.

The Bible does not say that we would not face problems, yet in whatever circumstance we find ourselves in, we must learn, in the words of the songwriter to say, "Whatever my lot, Thou has taught me to say, it is well with my soul". Weeping does go on for the whole night but since God has used the night to describe weeping, He has also set a boundary to weeping times in your life. Joy must follow with the breaking of day.

When that time comes for you to operate under the anointing of joy, you may not look like the right person to be blessed and highly favoured. You may not look like the obvious person to receive the kind of favour God has given. You may not look like the lady who should marry such a handsome man. You may not look like the man who should have the hand of such a pleasant lady.

If someone has an opinion that you may not qualify for the job you got, they probably have failed to realise:

You are a dream waiting to be fulfilled
Somebody's poem waiting to be recited
You are an unsung song
In the programme of God you are an unpublished book
You are of value, of great value

You are a vision waiting to be fulfilled
A future waiting to happen
You are a miracle waiting to break forth
You are a healing waiting to be received
You are a testimony waiting to be manifested
You are a prosperity waiting for its appropriate season to come forth

God does invade the affairs of men and if He has to invade your personal agenda to make all the aforesaid happen, then get ready for it. You may have to receive it in the posture of prayer.

> Call unto me, and I will answer thee, and shew thee great and mighty things, which thou knowest not.
> Jeremiah 33:3 (KJV)

Because when men make up their mind to receive from God and they ask, seek and knock. God has promised to make favours available to them.

> Ask, and it shall be given you; seek, and ye shall find; knock, and it shall be opened unto you:
> For every one that asketh receiveth; and he that seeketh findeth; and to him that knocketh it shall be opened.
> Matthew 7:7-8 (KJV)

There is a mercy beyond imagination to the man who has chosen to pray.

And therefore will the LORD wait, that he may be
gracious unto you, and therefore will he be exalted, that
he may have mercy upon you: for the LORD is a God
of judgment: blessed are all they that wait for him.
For the people shall dwell in Zion at Jerusalem: thou
shalt weep no more: he will be very gracious unto thee
at the voice of thy cry; when he shall hear it, he will
answer thee.
Isaiah 30:18-19 (KJV)

John Wesley, the founder of the Methodist Movement,
said the only thing which limits God is the limit of our
prayer. Smith Wigglesworth argues that the shuffling of
the leprous cannot stop them. The limitations of the
blind cannot stop them. There is something about
believing God in prayer that will cause God to pass a mil-
lion people to get to the praying man.

# THE PROBLEM BEFORE THE 24 HOUR MIRACLE

Our passage reveals:

## 1.    A famine that will not end

The people of God were confronted with an unusual famine. The drought which made people eat bird waste. A famine that had troubled the people of God, a famine which turned decent people into cannibals.

> And he said, If the LORD do not help thee, whence shall I help thee? out of the barnfloor, or out of the winepress? And the king said unto her, What aileth thee? And she answered, This woman said unto me, Give thy son, that we may eat him to day, and we will eat my son to morrow.
>
> 2 Kings 6:27-28 (KJV)

One of the reasons the enemy sets us up for certain problems is so that we can turn around and act out of character, so that we can turn around and act as if we did not know Christ.

The prodigal son in the story Jesus told encountered a famine he never expected. A famine is often symbolic of emptiness and dryness at the end of a life that is not God-glorifying. Famine was often used by God to discipline His people in the Old Testament and bring them in line with the will of God. Before the breakthrough, the possibilities are there that one could go through a famine period in his life.

Next we are confronted with:

## 2. The problem of unbelieving believers

Then a lord on whose hand the king leaned answered the man of God, and said, Behold, if the LORD would make windows in heaven, might this thing be? And he said, Behold, thou shalt see it with thine eyes, but shalt not eat thereof.
2 Kings 7:2 (KJV)

Jesus saith unto him, Thomas, because thou hast seen me, thou hast believed: blessed are they that have not seen, and yet have believed.
John 20:29 (KJV)

And when the child was grown, it fell on a day, that he went out to his father to the reapers.
2 Kings 4:18 (KJV)

This is a mirror of people who are in church, but not in

church. Almost saved, but not really saved. Not inside, but by the Beautiful Gate. They know about the Kingdom, they are used to the life of the Kingdom, but they have not found their way in.

Unbelieving believers hold on to agnostic opinions and ideas. Some may not go that far, they are close to the Kingdom, but they will always stop at the level of "almost".

> Then Agrippa said unto Paul, Almost thou persuadest
> me to be a Christian.
> Acts 26:28 (KJV)

Thirdly when problems persist they:

## 3. Turn people numb against God

In the story of 2 Kings 7 another set of characters playing out what happened here were four lepers. The statements they made seem to catergorise them.

The statement of the first of the four lepers makes him fit into the description of being:

## 1.    An Existentialist

> ... "Why are we sitting here until we die?
> 2 Kings 7:3 (NKJV)

Existentialism came out of a movement which started in the 20th Century and was influenced in its development by Kierkergaarde and Nietzsche and was popularised in France by Sartre. The philosophy of these three men has since highly influenced the subject of belief in Europe and across the world. The International Websters Comprehensive Dictionary of the English language defines existentialism as "The sum total of his acts, rather than his intention or potentialities and exists in order to win himself to act". In a nutshell he needs no other body, personality or being to determine his destiny. Neither is he accountable to anyone.

## 2. Annihilationist

"If we say we will enter the city, the famine is in the city
and we shall die there"
2 Kings 7:4a (NKJV)

Annihilation is that theological doctrine that the impenitent will be totally annihilated after death. In other words, following their departure from this earth, those who do not serve God will be annihilated and therefore will no longer exist or be elsewhere; either suffering the consequence of impenitence.

This view must have been held by this leper and others like him, in order to justify the troubles people go through, hoping that such a mind-set will help them escape the reality of the harshness of their situation.

Whereas, accountability in eternity is inevitable according to Scriptures in Hebrews 9:27.

> And as it is appointed unto men once to die, but after this the judgment:
> Hebrews 9:27 (KJV)

## 3.     Pessimist

> .. And if we sit here, we die also.
> 2 Kings 7:4 (NKJV)

There are no monuments built to pessimists. Pessimists water down your faith and make you give up easily. Pessimists look for easy ways out of every situation. The king's advisor was pessimistic about God's ability to provide. He did not see how God could cause such breakthrough and in such a short time.

> So an officer on whose hand the king leaned answered the man of God and said, "Look, if the LORD would make windows in heaven, could this thing be?" And he said, "In fact, you shall see it with your eyes, but you shall not eat of it."
> 2 Kings 7:2 (NKJV)

# THE PROCESS FOR THE 24 HOUR MIRACLE

Problems bring out people's strength or the lack of it. It reveals the ability already residing on the inside or the lack of it. Problems are intended to lead to a process. That is what God wants us to learn or do on our way to the miraculous which He wants to bring to pass in our life.

What is the process for the 24 hour miracle in this story? The first thing which we see of Elisha was his ability to:

## 1.    Hear God

Then Elisha said, "Hear the word of the LORD. Thus says the LORD: 'Tomorrow about this time a seah of fine flour shall be sold for a shekel, and two seahs of barley for a shekel, at the gate of Samaria.' "
2 Kings 7:1 (NKJV)

Those who hear God, speak His counsel and His mind. They hear what God is saying irrespective of what is going on around them. Those who hear God rise above certain circumstances. Those who hear God think like He does.

Your association determines your assilimation. The people you hang around determine the things you begin to hear and do.

For my thoughts are not your thoughts, neither are your ways my ways, saith the LORD. For as the heavens are higher than the earth, so are my ways higher than your ways, and my thoughts than your thoughts.
Isaiah 55:8-9 (KJV)

You must train your ears to hear God. Two brothers were walking down one of the busy streets of New York. The younger had come from the farmlands to visit his brother who lived in the city. Suddenly he stops to say he hears the sound of a cricket. His brother laughed at him and thought he was crazy to think that a cricket could be found on the busy streets of New York. The younger brother was persistent, he walked towards a little stone that was on the corner of the road as cars drove past and as he lifted the stone there truly was the cricket under the stone.

Those who are spiritually deaf will let the enemy take advantage of them.

I remember reading of an American evangelist who along with his associate who was a Native American had gone to visit the Niagara Falls and as he stood by the waterfall, the Native American suddenly asked the Evangelist to bend and hide in the bush because an enemy was approaching. The evangelist thought it could not be, he said, "How could you know that an enemy was coming?" There was no time to deliberate when suddenly he heard someone approaching. When the enemy had left, he asked the Native American how he knew of the approach. He said he heard the breaking of twigs. In a place where the sound of the waterfall was so loud that they could hardly hear each other; the Native American had trained his ear to hear the breaking of twigs.

If you are spiritually deaf you would miss a coming favour, you would miss the chance to know the mind of the Lord and to walk in His counsel.

## Spiritual deafness causes a man to act like a snake that will not hear the voice of the charmer.

It is time to train your ears to hear the voice of the Holy Spirit clearly and expressly.

Now the Spirit speaketh expressly, that in the latter times some shall depart from the faith, giving heed to seducing spirits, and doctrines of devils;
Speaking lies in hypocrisy; having their conscience seared with a hot iron;
1 Timothy 4:1-2 (KJV)

He that hath an ear, let him hear what the Spirit saith
unto the churches....
Revelation 2:7 (KJV)

Because if your ears are not picking what the Holy Spirit is saying, if your ears are not pick what God is strongly impressing, you will not be able to move in the seasons of blessing and favour which God is about to initiate and create for your life. If your radio is tuned to the wrong frequency you will pick a message different from what you intended. Israel tuned to the wrong frequency sent out by 10 spies, the result is devastating. Every adult who left Egypt died in the wilderness. If you listen and pay close attention, the ear of your Spirit will be open and you will be no longer misdirected by the voices around you. Imagine what would have happened if Abraham did not hear and obey the voice of the Lord. Certainly he would have missed his destiny and purpose.

## 2.    Hunger for God

Blessed are they which do hunger and thirst after
righteousness: for they shall be filled.
Matthew 5:6 (KJV)

Natural hunger is necessary for the health of our body, spiritual hunger is necessary for us to be able to flow with God.

Hunger for God opens the heart of God to you. Hunger for God opens the hand of God to you.

> .. for they shall be filled.
> Matthew 5:6 (KJV)

Such hunger comes by reason of experiencing the divine encounter with the presence of God. Hunger makes you to connect with God. Matthew 5:6 connects hunger and thirst, these are two natural expressions which are necessary to keep our body healthy. They are also necessary to keep our spirit connected to receive from God.

> As the hart panteth after the water brooks, so panteth my soul after thee, O God.
> Psalms 42:1 (KJV)

## 3. Live in the spirit realm

There was nothing to indicate a change in the economic realm on the occasion when Elisha prophesied, at least nothing in the natural, but in the spirit realm something was happening. The prophet has heard from above and not from what can be seen in the natural.

> While we look not at the things which are seen, but at the things which are not seen: for the things which are

seen are temporal; but the things which are not seen are
eternal.
2 Corinthians 4:18 (KJV)

I was in the Spirit on the Lord's day, and heard behind
me a great voice, as of a trumpet,
Revelation 1:10 (KJV)

The realm of the spirit is the place of spiritual awareness
where we become conscious of what God is saying,
doing and executing in this earthly realm. It is the place
about the awareness of the greatness and sweetness of
Jesus. It is the realm where the affairs of this world is
pre-determined. It is a place where the greatest battles
are already taking place before there is an earthly manifestation.

(For the weapons of our warfare are not carnal, but
mighty through God to the pulling down of strong
holds;) Casting down imaginations, and every high
thing that exalteth itself against the knowledge of God,
and bringing into captivity every thought to the
obedience of Christ;
2 Corinthians 10:4-5 (KJV)

It is a place of spiritual focus where God's people hear
Him, know Him and walk with Him. The realm of the
spirit is not some mystical place, nebulous or a plain of
nothingness. It is a place where when we are led by the
Spirit of God we can discover and follow the counsel of
the Lord.

This I say then, Walk in the Spirit, and ye shall not fulfil the lust of the flesh.

But if ye be led of the Spirit, ye are not under the law.

If we live in the Spirit, let us also walk in the Spirit.
Galatians 5:16, 18, 25 (KJV)

# ENTERING THE 24 HOUR MIRACLE

### 4.    Expectancy

The Bible account of this passage is of four lepers, we have seen three. The existentialist, the annihiliationist, the pessimist and now the fourth man. We had not previously mentioned him, but there is something different about him. It is my personal conviction that every time God wants to move in a geographical location, He is looking for a heart or a person that is accessible, amiable and available. It seems like God found the person in the fourth leper.

He had physical limitations but that was not going to stop him from becoming who he was called to be. He could only shuffle not even walk. Along with his friends, Levitical laws require that he announces his arrival as "Unclean, unclean". Bells around his clothes rang as he shuffled along with his friends. Mental, physical, emotional, social limitations were on this man. Like many of us have experienced at different times, yet he was marked by expectancy, and his expectation birthed manifestation.

Suddenly the 24 hour anointing became available and with a sense of expectancy of the fourth leper, God began to move upon the land. In expectation he turned and said to his friends I am sure, "Come let us go to the camp of the Assyrians".

> .. Now therefore, come, let us surrender to the army of the Syrians. If they keep us alive, we shall live; and if they kill us, we shall only die."
> 2 Kings 7:4 (NKJV)

The prophecy had gone forth the previous day that deliverance was in Zion and before the breaking of day, God had already found a faithful servant whom He would use to make good His Word. God's Word always operates as if it has a return ticket, but it would not apply that return ticket to the journey and go back until it has delivered the purpose for which it was sent.

> So shall my word be that goeth forth out of my mouth: it shall not return unto me void, but it shall accomplish that which I please, and it shall prosper in the thing whereto I sent it.
> Isaiah 55:11 (KJV)

When you walk in expectancy you give God a chance to move. When you walk in expectancy you have expressed trust and belief in His ability to walk and to do the miraculous.

The atmosphere of expectancy is the breeding ground of the miraculous. You need to talk it, you need to see it and the breakthrough will be there. When others say they do not see anything, you must express what you see in the mind of the Spirit.

While we look not at the things which are seen, but at the things which are not seen: for the things which are seen are temporal; but the things which are not seen are eternal.
2 Corinthians 4:18 (KJV)

Expectancy is the key to destroying depression. You must learn to see an ordained future that will cause a breaking forth of joy.

Expectancy means that you have not given up.

Expectancy means that you trust in the God that shows up when His people trust in Him, when they wait on Him.

And it shall be said in that day, Lo, this is our God; we have waited for him, and he will save us: this is the LORD; we have waited for him, we will be glad and rejoice in his salvation.
For in this mountain shall the hand
Isaiah 25:9-10 (KJV)

# Expectancy surrounds the birth of a baby.

When a woman is pregnant, we say she is expecting. We do not have a baby in our hands as yet, but we already have a name, we already have a celebration announced. There is a 24 hour anointing and you are pregnant with a miracle.

In the midst of the greatest famine, God sends forth a word that this time tomorrow:

In the next 24 hours there shall be a breakthrough

In the next 24 hours the enemy will be silenced.

In the next 24 hours you will receive the joy you desire

In the next 24 hours the doors that are closed will swing forth open by themselves.

In the next 24 hours your enemies will reconcile with you.

In the next 24 hours you will get that proposal you have been waiting for.

In the next 24 hours they would announce your name for favour.

In the next 24 hours, estates, properties, benefits will be coming your way.

What do you do if that is what God is cooking in the Spirit realm on your behalf? Act like a pregnant woman, act like your water is about to break. When a woman is expecting and she is close to the date when she is within 24 hours of her blessing, if you ask such a person to go somewhere, she will say,

"I can't go far, I feel something."
"I can't go far I have seen something."
"I can't go far I can deliver any time."

Act like you already know what to receive and therefore cannot go far. Act like you already know what to believe God for.

Within 24 hours the lepers came into:

## 1.    A season of powerful manifestations

And they rose up in the twilight, to go unto the camp of the Syrians: and when they were come to the uttermost part of the camp of Syria, behold, there was no man there. For the Lord had made the host of the Syrians to hear a noise of chariots, and a noise of horses, even the noise of a great host: and they said one to another, Lo, the king of Israel hath hired against us the kings of the Hittites, and the kings of the Egyptians, to come upon us. Wherefore they arose and fled in the twilight, and left their tents, and their horses, and their asses, even the camp as it was, and fled for their life.
2 Kings 7:5-7 (KJV)

The enemies have heard a mighty sound, to them it was the sound of a thundering army hired by Israel. God is humorous in His dealings, He had converted the shuffling of four lepers; three of them walking in unbelief. The annihilist, the existentialist and the pessimist, only one man, the fourth one walking in expectation. Now God had converted their simple shuffles to be like the sound of a mighty army.

> And he answered, Fear not: for they that be with us are more than they that be with them.
>
> 2 Kings 6:16 (KJV)

God is already fighting on your behalf, tearing down the walls the enemy built, pulling down strongholds which satan has brought. In the natural it seems as if your situation has not changed, but the anointing for the 24 hour miracle has gone forth. It cannot come back void.

## 2.    A day of prosperity to the full

> And when these lepers came to the uttermost part of the camp, they went into one tent, and did eat and drink, and carried thence silver, and gold, and raiment, and went and hid it; and came again, and entered into another tent, and carried thence also, and went and hid it.
>
> 2 Kings 7:8 (KJV)

The only memory the lepers had was of living from hand to mouth, having to depend on people's benevolence; crumbs that were thrown to them. But right now there is a release of an anointing that can take a man to levels he never thought. God has made the day, the day of a sudden full prosperity. All-round prosperity.

A twenty year old problem can turn around in one day when the 24 hour anointing is in motion.

Five years of trouble can end in a minute when the 24 hour anointing is in motion. The five years of trouble you have gone through in your marriage can become history when a 24 hour anointing is in motion. The five years of struggle in your relationships can end in a short while. The five years of trouble you have known in your finances can turn around in a few minutes because of the anointing of 24 hours, but you must walk in confident expectancy. The five years of trouble you have had of spiritual challenges can turn around anytime because of the 24 hour anointing.

So get ready for a change, get ready for an outburst of the favour of God on your life and family.
Get ready for a sudden breakthrough.
Get ready for a sudden turnaround.
Get ready for a sudden experience that will bring a testimony you have never known.

Four lepers, who were nobodies in the sight of men, yet they came into:

## 3.    A prepared blessing

And when these lepers came to the uttermost part of the camp, they went into one tent, and did eat and

drink, and carried thence silver, and gold, and raiment, and went and hid it; and came again, and entered into another tent, and carried thence also, and went and hid it.
2 Kings 7:8 (KJV)

Behold, the days come, saith the LORD, that the plowman shall overtake the reaper, and the treader of grapes him that soweth seed; and the mountains shall drop sweet wine, and all the hills shall melt.
Amos 9:13 (KJV)

For the seed shall be prosperous; the vine shall give her fruit, and the ground shall give her increase, and the heavens shall give their dew; and I will cause the remnant of this people to possess all these things.
And it shall come to pass, that as ye were a curse among the heathen, O house of Judah, and house of Israel; so will I save you, and ye shall be a blessing: fear not, but let your hands be strong.
Zech 8:12-13 (KJV)

Thou preparest a table before me in the presence of mine enemies: thou anointest my head with oil; my cup runneth over.
Psalms 23:5 (KJV)

Nothing is as enjoyable as a breakthrough you know was not delivered by your labour. It is nice to experience financial increase by way of interest from your bank, but there is a beauty to God opening unusual doors that causes you to come into financial progress which exceeds the interest of any bank and which you had nothing to do with except that you expected God to move on your behalf.

## 4.     They came into personal vision enlargement

For the vision is yet for an appointed time, but at the end it shall speak, and not lie: though it tarry, wait for it; because it will surely come, it will not tarry.
Habakkuk 2:3 (KJV)

What dream would a leper have at a time when there were no cures. What vision, what expectation? Other than to live from day to day and hope to die and go to heaven, but today God changed their mourning to dancing. He gave them beauty for their ashes and joy for their tears As you read this book, may the 24 hour anointing trigger an enlargement of your vision.

## 5. They came into the promised land of blessing and victory

And they went after them unto Jordan: and, lo, all the way was full of garments and vessels, which the Syrians had cast away in their haste. And the messengers returned, and told the king. And the people went out, and spoiled the tents of the Syrians. So a measure of fine flour was sold for a shekel, and two measures of barley for a shekel, according to the word of the LORD.
2 Kings 7:15-16 (KJV)

In spite of your weakness and inability to do many things, in spite of the limitations that are known to surround your life; a lack of adequate education, a lack of social connections, a lack of sufficient finances to carry out your vision. Get ready for God to move so fast in your life, in your home, in your business, in your ministry, in your work.

Something is about to break which nobody can stop in your life and the speed of your movement will defy expert opinion.

Those who hear it will simply think you are making up a story. In the case of these lepers, it was so fast that the king could not believe his ears. He said,

And the king arose in the night, and said unto his servants, I will now shew you what the Syrians have done to us. They know that we be hungry; therefore are they gone out of the camp to hide themselves in the field, saying, When they come out of the city, we shall catch them alive, and get into the city. And one of his servants answered and said, Let some take, I pray thee, five of the horses that remain, which are left in the city, (behold, they are as all the multitude of Israel that are left in it: behold, I say, they are even as all the multitude of the Israelites that are consumed:) and let us send and see. They took therefore two chariot horses; and the king sent after the host of the Syrians, saying, Go and see.   2 Kings 7:12-14 (KJV)

The time and season has come in your life when the weeping that has been for a night would change to the morning glory, the joy of the morning. You will operate under the 24 hour anointing, when suddenly God Himself will break upon your situation. The Bible will often use the word "suddenly". This word means hastily, quickly and without warning. Get ready for a breakthrough that will come upon your life hastily, quickly and without warning. Get ready because those who expect nothing get a lot of it. Get ready, expect exceeding abundantly.

Now to Him who, by (in consequence of) [action of His] power that is at work within us, is able to (carry out His purpose and) do superabundantly, far over and above all that we [dare] ask or think [infinitely beyond our highest prayers, desires, thoughts, hopes or dreams].
Ephesians 3:20 (Amp)

Get ready for it to come hastily, quickly and without warning.

CHAPTER 3

# MORDECAI

## From bondage to breakthrough

What is man, that thou art mindful of him? and the
son of man, that thou visitest him?
For thou hast made him a little lower than the angels,
and hast crowned him with glory and honour.
Psalms 8:4-5 (KJV)

You must know that satan cannot stand you because
you exist to pleasure God.

Thou art worthy, O Lord, to receive glory and honour
and power: for thou hast created all things, and for thy
pleasure they are and were created.
Revelation 4:11 (KJV)

We pleasure Him because we are His image. We worship
Him, we exalt His name, we give Him the highest praise.
This was an opportunity satan had previously, but now he
does not because he lost his place. This loss of position
and God directing His affection towards humanity, makes
satan to bring the battle to our door.

We are in a war, battles are part of the Christian walk. The arrival of the Israelites in Canaan is not symbolic of movement to heaven. It is symbolic of movement from being unsaved into the Christian life, just like they fought battles in Canaan to possess their possession, we are exposed to battle in order to know the victorious Christian life. It is only in heaven that we become the church triumphant.

It is with this battle in sight that Paul warned Timothy to tell him to remember that as a soldier he must not be carried away by civilian life.

Thou therefore endure hardness, as a good soldier of Jesus Christ.
2 Timothy 2:3 (KJV)

Also, it is into this battle that we are given the assurance in the Scriptures that if we fight right we have victory.

Now thanks be unto God, which always causeth us to triumph in Christ, and maketh manifest the savour of his knowledge by us in every place.
2 Corinthians 2:14 (KJV)

But the reality of the battle we face pales in the victory we are assured of. We are not the force behind our victory. God is. We cannot throw our hands in the air as if to celebrate our ability to make it happen. God is the one who causes us to know victory through the Lord

Jesus Christ.

# When the battles come, they only introduce us into a breakthrough God has already prepared.

So you will not outgrow warfare, you would only use it as your stepping-stone to the miraculous. How matters look now must not disturb what it shall like be when you finally win.

> When thou passest through the waters, I will be with thee; and through the rivers, they shall not overflow thee: when thou walkest through the fire, thou shalt not be burned; neither shall the flame kindle upon thee.
> Isaiah 43:2 (KJV)

Those obstacles the enemy threw before you must be used as stepping-stones by you into the things God has for you. Battles come as you make effort to fulfil the destiny you were ordained for. You will win. Yet firstly you must face:

> So the king and Haman came to banquet with Esther the queen. And the king said again unto Esther on the second day at the banquet of wine, What is thy petition, queen Esther? and it shall be granted thee: and what is thy request? and it shall be performed, even to the half of the kingdom. Then Esther the queen answered and said, If I have found favour in thy sight, O king, and if

it please the king, let my life be given me at my petition, and my people at my request: For we are sold, I and my people, to be destroyed, to be slain, and to perish. But if we had been sold for bondmen and bondwomen, I had held my tongue, although the enemy could not countervail the king's damage. Then the king Ahasuerus answered and said unto Esther the queen, Who is he, and where is he, that durst presume in his heart to do so? And Esther said, The adversary and enemy is this wicked Haman. Then Haman was afraid before the king and the queen. And the king arising from the banquet of wine in his wrath went into the palace garden: and Haman stood up to make request for his life to Esther the queen; for he saw that there was evil determined against him by the king. Then the king returned out of the palace garden into the place of the banquet of wine; and Haman was fallen upon the bed whereon Esther was. Then said the king, Will he force the queen also before me in the house? As the word went out of the king's mouth, they covered Haman's face. And Harbonah, one of the chamberlains, said before the king, Behold also, the gallows fifty cubits high, which Haman had made for Mordecai, who had spoken good for the king, standeth in the house of Haman. Then the king said, Hang him thereon. So they hanged Haman on the gallows that he had prepared for Mordecai. Then was the king's wrath pacified.

Esther 7:1-10 (KJV)

On that day did the king Ahasuerus give the house of
Haman the Jews' enemy unto Esther the queen. And
Mordecai came before the king; for Esther had told
what he was unto her. And the king took off his ring,
which he had taken from Haman, and gave it unto
Mordecai. And Esther set Mordecai over the house of
Haman. And Esther spake yet again before the king, and
fell down at his feet, and besought him with tears to put
away the mischief of Haman the Agagite, and his device
that he had devised against the Jews. Then the king
held out the golden sceptre toward Esther. So Esther
arose, and stood before the king, And said, If it please
the king, and if I have found favour in his sight, and the
thing seem right before the king, and I be pleasing in his
eyes, let it be written to reverse the letters devised by
Haman the son of Hammedatha the Agagite, which he
wrote to destroy the Jews which are in all the king's
provinces: For how can I endure to see the evil that
shall come unto my people? or how can I endure to see
the destruction of my kindred? Then the king
Ahasuerus said unto Esther the queen and to Mordecai
the Jew, Behold, I have given Esther the house of
Haman, and him they have hanged upon the gallows,
because he laid his hand upon the Jews. Write ye also
for the Jews, as it liketh you, in the king's name, and seal
it with the king's ring: for the writing which is written in
the king's name, and sealed with the king's ring, may no
man reverse. Then were the king's scribes called at that
time in the third month, that is, the month Sivan, on the
three and twentieth day thereof; and it was written

according to all that Mordecai commanded unto the Jews, and to the lieutenants, and the deputies and rulers of the provinces which are from India unto Ethiopia, an hundred twenty and seven provinces, unto every province according to the writing thereof, and unto every people after their language, and to the Jews according to their writing, and according to their language. And he wrote in the king Ahasuerus' name, and sealed it with the king's ring, and sent letters by posts on horseback, and riders on mules, camels, and young dromedaries: Wherein the king granted the Jews which were in every city to gather themselves together, and to stand for their life, to destroy, to slay, and to cause to perish, all the power of the people and province that would assault them, both little ones and women, and to take the spoil of them for a prey, Upon one day in all the provinces of king Ahasuerus, namely, upon the thirteenth day of the twelfth month, which is the month Adar. The copy of the writing for a commandment to be given in every province was published unto all people, and that the Jews should be ready against that day to avenge themselves on their enemies. So the posts that rode upon mules and camels went out, being hastened and pressed on by the king's commandment. And the decree was given at Shushan the palace. And Mordecai went out from the presence of the king in royal apparel of blue and white, and with a great crown of gold, and with a garment of fine linen and purple: and the city of Shushan rejoiced and was glad. The Jews had light, and gladness, and joy, and honour. And in every province, and in every city, whithersoever the king's commandment and his decree came, the Jews had joy and gladness, a feast and a good day. And many of the people of the land became Jews; for the fear of the Jews fell upon them.

Esther 8:1-17 (KJV)

# THE PROBLEMS BEFORE THE BREAKTHROUGH

## 1.     Slavery

Israel's disobedience meant that they were taken into servitude. The people of God were now taken into captivity and had to serve by the rivers of Babylon, where they remembered Zion.

> By the rivers of Babylon, there we sat down, yea, we wept, when we remembered Zion.
> Psalms 137:1 (KJV)

God had already warned them that if they disobeyed Him, instead of them being above their enemies, they would rather be taken by their enemies into captivity.

> Thou shalt beget sons and daughters, but thou shalt not enjoy them; for they shall go into captivity.
> Deuteronomy 28:41 (KJV)

> The LORD shall bring a nation against thee from far, from the end of the earth, as swift as the eagle flieth; a nation whose tongue thou shalt not understand;

A nation of fierce countenance, which shall not regard
the person of the old, nor shew favour to the young:
And he shall eat the fruit of thy cattle, and the fruit of
thy land, until thou be destroyed: which also shall not
leave thee either corn, wine, or oil, or the increase of
thy kine, or flocks of thy sheep, until he have destroyed
thee. And he shall besiege thee in all thy gates, until thy
high and fenced walls come down, wherein thou trust-
edst, throughout all thy land: and he shall besiege thee in
all thy gates throughout all thy land, which the LORD
thy God hath given thee.
Deuteronomy 28:49-52 (KJV)

Disobedience still causes economic, spiritual, physical,
mental and emotional slavery. It was from such slavery
that Jesus came to redeem us.

Ye are bought with a price; be not ye the servants of
men.
1 Corinthians 7:23 (KJV)

## 2.    Humiliation

Because they were in slavery they had to do every menial
job passed on to them. They had to accept whatever the
taskmasters placed on them. Though Mordecai was full
of wisdom, he found himself being a gatekeeper. There
was nothing anyone could do for him, not even his niece;
the queen of the land.

## 3.    Hatred

The degree of hatred expressed at them in the times of Esther may have not been clear to us, but it is obvious from Haman's hatred for the Jews, that there must have been so much hatred against the people of God that Haman was ready to pay for the annihilation of Mordecai.

> And Haman said unto king Ahasuerus, There is a certain people scattered abroad and dispersed among the people in all the provinces of thy kingdom; and their laws are diverse from all people; neither keep they the king's laws: therefore it is not for the king's profit to suffer them. If it please the king, let it be written that they may be destroyed: and I will pay ten thousand talents of silver to the hands of those that have the charge of the business, to bring it into the king's treasuries.    And the king took his ring from his hand, and gave it unto Haman the son of Hammedatha the Agagite, the Jews' enemy.  And the king said unto Haman, The silver is given to thee, the people also, to do with them as it seemeth good to thee.
> Esther 3:8-11 (KJV)

Mordecai was hated because he would not quake before man.

Then went Haman forth that day joyful and with a glad heart: but when Haman saw Mordecai in the king's gate,

that he stood not up, nor moved for him, he was full of
indignation against Mordecai. Nevertheless Haman
refrained himself: and when he came home, he sent and
called for his friends, and Zeresh his wife. And Haman
told them of the glory of his riches, and the multitude
of his children, and all the things wherein the king had
promoted him, and how he had advanced him above the
princes and servants of the king. Haman said
moreover, Yea, Esther the queen did let no man come
in with the king unto the banquet that she had prepared
but myself; and to morrow am I invited unto her also
with the king. Yet all this availeth me nothing, so long
as I see Mordecai the Jew sitting at the king's gate.
Esther 5:9-13 (KJV)

## 4.    Genocide

Haman was probably one of the first in history to plan
ethnic cleansing against the Jews. He planned for their
destruction from the face of the earth, so that the
prophetic word given to Abraham would not be fulfilled.

Now the LORD had said unto Abram, Get thee out of
thy country, and from thy kindred, and from thy father's
house, unto a land that I will shew thee: And I will
make of thee a great nation, and I will bless thee, and
make thy name great; and thou shalt be a blessing:
Genesis 12:1-2 (KJV)

Yet it does not matter what instrument the enemy applies,
once God's prophetic Word has gone forth, it never
returns to Him void.

## 5.    Hanging

Haman also planned the destruction of Mordecai. Mordecai in this story was the carrier of God's purpose.

> Then said Zeresh his wife and all his friends unto him, Let a gallows be made of fifty cubits high, and to morrow speak thou unto the king that Mordecai may be hanged thereon: then go thou in merrily with the king unto the banquet. And the thing pleased Haman; and he caused the gallows to be made.
> Esther 5:14 (KJV)

The intensity of the battle you face is an indication of the destiny you carry.  No one wastes his raw material fighting an enemy that is not of any concern.

# THE PROCESS

We have established in every one of the cases we have considered, the fact that you must go through a process before you come into the 24 hour miracle.

God's process lines you up for the favour you are about to receive. It gets you in motion for the breakthrough God is about to bring to your life. God was about to move in a special way for Esther and Mordecai, but in particular for Mordecai.

A man of a lowly estate, albeit intense wisdom, who God would show great victory and make to progress so rapidly. Not because of human connection, but Godly intervention. From the story of Esther and Mordecai, we see:

## a.    You must understand your purpose

Having been brought into Babylonian captivity, and having won the beauty contest in the palace of Ahaseurus it was necessary that Mordecai remind Esther that she was an ambassador to the palace; not to be carried away by the prestige of the position but the purpose she represented. When purpose is not known the certainty is that abuse will follow.

One of the worst things that can happen to you is to have no one who can speak into your life and remind you to walk in the purpose for which you were called.

> For if thou altogether holdest thy peace at this time, then shall there enlargement and deliverance arise to the Jews from another place; but thou and thy father's house shall be destroyed: and who knoweth whether thou art come to the kingdom for such a time as this?
> Esther 4:14 (KJV)

God's great and eternal purpose overrides every other reason for our being on this planet. It is greater than what was on our parents mind when they decided to have us.

Purpose nullifies the thought that you were a product of somebody's sexual prowess. It nullifies the thought that you are an accident of pro-creation.

## b.     You must understand the power of fasting

> Then Esther bade them return Mordecai this answer, Go, gather together all the Jews that are present in Shushan, and fast ye for me, and neither eat nor drink three days, night or day: I also and my maidens will fast likewise;....     Esther 4:15-16 (KJV)

With the challenge looming over Israel, the enemy threatening to exterminate them from the face of the earth, she knew that this kind of problem cannot just disappear by wishing. When they brought a child before Jesus and His disciples could not cast out the demon, Jesus said, "This kind goeth not out, expect by praying and fasting"

And he said unto them, This kind can come forth by nothing, but by prayer and fasting.
Mark 9:29 (KJV)

What does fasting do?

## 1.   Fasting humbles the soul before God

But as for me, when they were sick, my clothing was sackcloth: I humbled my soul with fasting; and my prayer returned into mine own bosom.
Psalms 35:13 (KJV)

## 2.   It chastens the heart that may have strayed from the purpose of God and therefore needs to repent

When I wept, and chastened my soul with fasting, that was to my reproach.
I made sackcloth also my garment; and I became a proverb to them.
Psalms 69:10-11 (KJV)

## 3. It crucifies the fleshly appetites, so we can focus on prayer

David therefore besought God for the child; and David
fasted, and went in, and lay all night upon the earth.
And the elders of his house arose, and went to him, to
raise him up from the earth: but he would not, neither
did he eat bread with them. And it came to pass on the
seventh day, that the child died. And the servants of
David feared to tell him that the child was dead: for they
said, Behold, while the child was yet alive, we spake unto
him, and he would not hearken unto our voice: how will
he then vex himself, if we tell him that the child is dead?
But when David saw that his servants whispered, David
perceived that the child was dead: therefore David said
unto his servants, Is the child dead? And they said, He is
dead. Then David arose from the earth, and washed,
and anointed himself, and changed his apparel, and
came into the house of the LORD, and worshipped:
then he came to his own house; and when he required,
they set bread before him, and he did eat. Then said his
servants unto him, What thing is this that thou hast
done? thou didst fast and weep for the child, while it
was alive; but when the child was dead, thou didst rise
and eat bread. And he said, While the child was yet alive,
I fasted and wept: for I said, Who can tell whether
GOD will be gracious to me, that the child may live?
But now he is dead, wherefore should I fast? can I bring
him back again? I shall go to him, but he shall not
return to me.     2 Samuel 12:16-23 (KJV)

But Daniel purposed in his heart that he would not defile himself with the portion of the king's meat, nor with the wine which he drank: therefore he requested of the prince of the eunuchs that he might not defile himself.
Daniel 1:8 (KJV)

## 4.   It expresses earnestness and zeal before God to the exclusion of all else

Defraud ye not one the other, except it be with consent for a time, that ye may give yourselves to fasting and prayer; and come together again, that Satan tempt you not for your incontinency.
1 Corinthians 7:5 (KJV)

## 5.   It is a source of freedom from all bondage

Is not this the fast that I have chosen? to loose the bands of wickedness, to undo the heavy burdens, and to let the oppressed go free, and that ye break every yoke?
Isaiah 58:6 (KJV)

## 6.   It brings salvation for loved ones

Is it not to deal thy bread to the hungry, and that thou bring the poor that are cast out to thy house? when thou seest the naked, that thou cover him; and that thou hide not thyself from thine own flesh?
Isaiah 58:7 (KJV)

## 7.    Healing

Then shall thy light break forth as the morning, and
thine health shall spring forth speedily: and thy righteousness shall go before thee; the glory of the LORD
shall be thy rereward.

Isaiah 58:8 (KJV)

## 8.    Glory

Then shall thy light break forth as the morning, and
thine health shall spring forth speedily: and thy righteousness shall go before thee; the glory of the LORD
shall be thy rereward.

Isaiah 58:8 (KJV)

Strongs concordance of Hebrew/Greek - No 3519D
defines 'Glory' from the Hebrew word 'kabod' as:

> Abundance
> Honour
> Glorious
> To be honourable
> Honoured
> Riches
> Splendid
> Splendour
> Wealth

All these follow after a period of denying oneself in the

presence of God in fasting.

## 9. Answered prayer

Then shalt thou call, and the LORD shall answer; thou shalt cry, and he shall say, Here I am. If thou take away from the midst of thee the yoke, the putting forth of the finger, and speaking vanity;
Isaiah 58:9 (KJV)

## 10. Divine Direction

And the LORD shall guide thee continually, and satisfy thy soul in drought, and make fat thy bones: and thou shalt be like a watered garden, and like a spring of water, whose waters fail not.
Isaiah 58:11 (KJV)

## 11. Prosperity

… and thou shalt be like a watered garden, and like a spring of water, whose waters fail not.
Isaiah 58:11b (KJV)

## 12. To possess the future

For I know the thoughts that I think toward you, saith the LORD, thoughts of peace, and not of evil, to give you an expected end.
Jeremiah 29:11 (KJV)

## 13.    Restoration

And I will restore to you the years that the locust hath
eaten, the cankerworm, and the caterpiller, and the
palmerworm, my great army which I sent among you.
And ye shall eat in plenty, and be satisfied, and praise
the name of the LORD your God, that hath dealt
wondrously with you: and my people shall never be
ashamed.  And ye shall know that I am in the midst of
Israel, and that I am the LORD your God, and none
else: and my people shall never be ashamed.
Joel 2:25-27 (KJV)

If the theft be certainly found in his hand alive, whether
it be ox, or ass, or sheep; he shall restore double.
Exodus 22:4 (KJV)

If my people, which are called by my name, shall
humble themselves, and pray, and seek my face, and turn
from their wicked ways; then will I hear from heaven,
and will forgive their sin, and will heal their land.
2 Chronicles 7:14 (KJV)

## 14.    Devotion

Fasting helps us in our seasons of waiting on God to be
devoted and to humble ourselves before God.  It makes
us to have our face set towards heaven and not be
distracted.

For the Lord GOD will help me; therefore shall I not
be confounded: therefore have I set my face like a flint,
and I know that I shall not be ashamed.
Isaiah 50:7 (KJV)

## 15.    Deliverance

And he said unto them, This kind can come forth by
nothing, but by prayer and fasting.
Mark 9:29 (KJV)

And if thou draw out thy soul to the hungry, and
satisfy the afflicted soul; then shall thy light rise in
obscurity, and thy darkness be as the noonday:
Isaiah 58:10 (KJV)

It is inevitable that we must understand there is a
connection between the prayer for deliverance and the
ability to wait on God in fasting.

## 16.    Subjection of the body

And every man that striveth for the mastery is temperate in all things. Now they do it to obtain a corruptible
crown; but we an incorruptible.  I therefore so run, not
as uncertainly; so fight I, not as one that beateth the air:
But I keep under my body, and bring it into subjection:
lest that by any means, when I have preached to others,
I myself should be a castaway.
1 Corinthians 9:25-27 (KJV)

## 17.    Power (Anointing)

> And, being assembled together with them, commanded
> them that they should not depart from Jerusalem, but
> wait for the promise of the Father, which, saith he, ye
> have heard of me.
> Acts 1:4 (KJV)

### c.    You must understand the power of prayer

Preceding the 24 hour miracle the believer must recognise the potency of prayer. God does nothing but in answer to believing prayer. So Esther called for warfare prayer, the kind of prayer that brings about the birthing of the miraculous.

> No man that warreth entangleth himself with the
> affairs of this life; that he may please him who hath
> chosen him to be a soldier.
> 2 Timothy 2:4 (KJV)

Prayer changes situations, prayer changes things, and prayer is God's battle-axe for tearing down the kingdom of satan. It is the humble cry of any saint that God will never overlook. If God can feed the animals and feed the ravens that cry, He would not turn His ears away from saints who call upon Him.

Prayer birthed in aggression and bold military stance brings forth a change. Such prayer must be intensive. As Joshua stood in the plains of Canaan, he commanded the sun and the moon to stand still. The Bible says, "...and God hearkened to the voice of a man, as He has never done before." It was prayer that got God's attention.

And there was no day like that before it or after it, that the LORD hearkened unto the voice of a man: for the LORD fought for Israel.
Joshua 10:14 (KJV)

Prayer swings down and upholds the world to immediate action. We are called to intense and fervent prayer in Scripture.

Confess your faults one to another, and pray one for another, that ye may be healed. The effectual fervent prayer of a righteous man availeth much.
James 5:16 (KJV)

You must recognise that the prayer energised by the Holy Spirit causes you to manifest an intensity in your commitment. Esther called for such intense prayer because the destiny of the Jews was at stake. It was such intense prayer that made a definite difference. Prayer must be with passion or else it does not produce results.

> Confess your faults one to another, and pray one for another, that ye may be healed. The effectual fervent prayer of a righteous man availeth much.
> James 5:16 (KJV)

It is prayer beyond the normal. It was the kind of prayer Jesus offered in the garden of Gethsemane when His sweat was like the dropping of blood.

## Powerful prayer produces powerful results.

She asked for an incessant pleading until the result came. The tragedy of the 21st century Christian is giving up too soon before there is a change.

We must travail so we can give birth to a miracle. Those who learn to travail come into the experience of prevailing. Intense prayer is your indication that you need a divine intervention.

### d. You must understand the power of intervention.

> .... and so will I go in unto the king, which is not according to the law: and if I perish, I perish.
> Esther 4:16 (KJV)

The BAS translation puts it as "and if death is to be my fate, let it come."

The Living Bible puts it as "if I must die, I am ready to die".

Esther recognised the fact that change does not come unless there is a determination. Whatever you are not determined about may never change.

## e. It is time to remember God's covenant commitment to you

God is committed to those who believe in Him to provide for them.

I have been young, and now am old; yet have I not seen
the righteous forsaken, nor his seed begging bread.
Psalms 37:25 (KJV)

His commitment is also to preserve them in the times of trouble.

The LORD will strengthen him upon the bed of languishing: thou wilt make all his bed in his sickness.
Psalms 41:3 (KJV)

Cast thy burden upon the LORD, and he shall sustain
thee: he shall never suffer the righteous to be moved.
Psalms 55:22 (KJV)

In spite of them being in slavery, God was committed to preserving them.

His commitment was also to protect.

I will say of the LORD, He is my refuge and my
fortress: my God; in him will I trust. Surely he shall
deliver thee from the snare of the fowler, and from the
noisome pestilence. He shall cover thee with his feath-
ers, and under his wings shalt thou trust: his truth shall
be thy shield and buckler. Thou shalt not be afraid for
the terror by night; nor for the arrow that flieth by day;
Nor for the pestilence that walketh in darkness; nor for
the destruction that wasteth at noonday.
A thousand shall fall at thy side, and ten thousand at thy
right hand; but it shall not come nigh thee.
Only with thine eyes shalt thou behold and see the
reward of the wicked.
Psalms 91:2-8 (KJV)


Trouble may have gone on for a long time as it did in
Babylon. Trouble may seem to last for long, but it
cannot last forever because God's ability to turn reverse
situations around is what makes Him God to us. Yet
satan has a way of acting like he has the upper hand, even
though he does not.

# THE 24 HOUR MIRACLE

The heat of adversity becomes the breeding ground for God's intervention. Haman was breathing fire; satan was having a field day. It seemed as if the future of the people of God was fixed for destruction, but Mordecai was willing to pay the price and go through the process. Esther was also willing to pay the price and go through the process and by that act they prepared themselves to come into an unusual anointing of the 24 hour miracle.

The first of which was, as the power of God broke upon Esther and Mordecai, and favour began to flow in that direction they experienced:

## 1. Uncommon access to decision-makers

Then Esther the queen answered and said, If I have found favour in thy sight, O king, and if it please the king, let my life be given me at my petition, and my people at my request: For we are sold, I and my people, to be destroyed, to be slain, and to perish. But if we had been sold for bondmen and bondwomen, I had held my tongue, although the enemy could not countervail the king's damage.
Esther 7:3-4 (KJV)

Slaves in the land suddenly had an audience with the king, given the privilege to speak to the one person in the land who could make decisions about them. When the 24 hour miracle breaks upon you, it gives you uncommon access.

## 2. The opportunity to see the enemy hanging on the trap he set

And Harbonah, one of the chamberlains, said before the king, Behold also, the gallows fifty cubits high, which Haman had made for Mordecai, who had spoken good for the king, standeth in the house of Haman. Then the king said, Hang him thereon. So they hanged Haman on the gallows that he had prepared for Mordecai. Then was the king's wrath pacified.
Esther 7:9-10 (KJV)

The trap which the enemy set had worked against him, all in 24 hours.

## 3. God moved Mordecai from an ordinary gatekeeper to the king's presence by reason of an uncommon relationship

For promotion cometh neither from the east, nor from the west, nor from the south.
Psalms 75:6 (KJV)

He raiseth up the poor out of the dust, and lifteth up
the beggar from the dunghill, to set them among
princes, and to make them inherit the throne of glory:
for the pillars of the earth are the LORD'S, and he hath
set the world upon them.
1 Samuel 2:8 (KJV)

## 4.    A transfer of authority from Haman to Mordecai

Within 24 hours the gateman had taken the place of the
man who seemed to be the prime minister of the land.
Mordecai, the despised and forsaken had become a man
of authority.  God had given him uncommon favour to
operate with power.

And the king took off his ring, which he had taken
from Haman, and gave it unto Mordecai. And Esther
set Mordecai over the house of Haman.
Esther 8:2 (KJV)

Within 24 hours God is able to bring you into the realm
of operating with authority.

But as for the mighty man, he had the earth; and the
honourable man dwelt in it.
Job 22:8 (KJV)

Verily I say unto you, Whatsoever ye shall bind on earth
shall be bound in heaven: and whatsoever ye shall loose
on earth shall be loosed in heaven.
Matthew 18:18 (KJV)

These things come with graduating in the grace of God
and yet it happened in Mordecai's life in 24 hours.

## 5.    There was a transfer of the riches of the wicked from Haman to Mordecai

And the king took off his ring, which he had taken
from Haman, and gave it unto Mordecai. And Esther
set Mordecai over the house of Haman.
Esther 8:2 (KJV)

God can break upon your situation and make you to suck
the breast of kings.  God can expose the hidden riches of
the dark places within a short time and bring you into a
realm of favour and wealth beyond you have ever known.

And I will give thee the treasures of darkness, and
hidden riches of secret places, that thou mayest know
that I, the LORD, which call thee by thy name, am the
God of Israel.
Isaiah 45:3 (KJV)

In Bible times when you inherited a man's house you also
inherited the occupants, his wife and children, his slaves

and servants, his goods and services.

## 6.    He came into unlimited power to bind and loose

Write ye also for the Jews, as it liketh you, in the king's name, and seal it with the king's ring: for the writing which is written in the king's name, and sealed with the king's ring, may no man reverse.
Esther 8:8 (KJV)

A displaced people within 24 hours had such power to permit things or to disallow, to give life or withdraw it.

## 7.    The power to decree a thing and for it to be established was given to him

See, I have this day set thee over the nations and over the kingdoms, to root out, and to pull down, and to destroy, and to throw down, to build, and to plant.
Jeremiah 1:10 (KJV)

(For the weapons of our warfare are not carnal, but mighty through God to the pulling down of strong holds;)
2 Corinthians 10:4 (KJV)

Thou shalt also decree a thing, and it shall be
established unto thee: and the light shall shine upon thy
ways.
Job 22:28 (KJV)

To bind their kings with chains, and their nobles with
fetters of iron;
Psalms 149:8 (KJV)

## 8.    Operating under a new authority, an unlimited authority

They shall take up serpents; and if they drink any deadly
thing, it shall not hurt them; they shall lay hands on the
sick, and they shall recover.  So then after the Lord had
spoken unto them, he was received up into heaven, and
sat on the right hand of God. And they went forth, and
preached every where, the Lord working with them, and
confirming the word with signs following. Amen.
Mark 16:18-20 (KJV)

All this happened within 24 hours as God breaks upon
His children and shows them favour.

## 9. Uncommon access to the kings best provisions

So the posts that rode upon mules and camels went
out, being hastened and pressed on by the king's
commandment. And the decree was given at Shushan
the palace.    Esther 8:14 (KJV)

If ye be willing and obedient, ye shall eat the good of
the land:
Isaiah 1:19 (KJV)

Thou hast caused men to ride over our heads; we went
through fire and through water: but thou broughtest us
out into a wealthy place.
Psalms 66:12 (KJV)

When a man's way begins to please the Lord and God
causes a 24 hour breakthrough to come upon him, these
are the favours he receives.

## 10.    God replaces your ashes with beauty

And Mordecai went out from the presence of the king
in royal apparel of blue and white, and with a great
crown of gold, and with a garment of fine linen and
purple: and the city of Shushan rejoiced and was glad.
Esther 8:15 (KJV)

You go from a pauper's look to the beauty of royalty as
you represent the King of kings.

## 11.    From gateman to a crowned man

..... and with a great crown of gold, and with a
garment of fine linen and purple: and the city of
Shushan rejoiced and was glad.
Esther 8:15 (KJV)

## 12. Operating in a new kind of joy and gladness

The Jews had light, and gladness, and joy, and honour.
Esther 8:16 (KJV)

Within 24 hours, a people who have bowed their head in fasting, have been brought into a season of joy and gladness.

## 13. A contagious blessing that surprises everyone around

Within 24 hours Mordecai was operating in a new dimension.

Ever since the fall of man, it had been satan's plan to sever God's relationship with man to disrupt the programme of salvation. He started his plan of ·destruction from a long time. But God always rescued His people, so that the course and destiny He had fixed would come to pass.

Herod tried to slaughter the infants of Bethlehem that he may kill Christ, but the word was sent and you cannot be killed. Satan tempted Christ to denounce God and worship him, but Christ was focused. Even Peter, a servant of Jesus Christ, at satan's insistence tried to block Jesus from dying for mankind, but the devil could not stop him.

Then Peter took him, and began to rebuke him, saying,
Be it far from thee, Lord: this shall not be unto thee.
Matthew 16:22 (KJV)

Finally satan took charge of another of his disciples in
the person of Judas, to try to frustrate the programme
God had, but it did not work.

In the book of Esther, satan's diabolical programme was
to destroy this people. They tried to jeopardise all of the
promises God had made to His people.

And when Abram was ninety years old and nine, the
LORD appeared to Abram, and said unto him, I am the
Almighty God; walk before me, and be thou perfect.

And I will give unto thee, and to thy seed after thee, the
land wherein thou art a stranger, all the land of Canaan,
for an everlasting possession; and I will be their God.
Genesis 17:1,8 (KJV)

And from Betah, and from Berothai, cities of
Hadadezer, king David took exceeding much brass.
When Toi king of Hamath heard that David had
smitten all the host of Hadadezer, Then Toi sent Joram
his son unto king David, to salute him, and to bless him,
because he had fought against Hadadezer, and smitten
him: for Hadadezer had wars with Toi. And Joram
brought with him vessels of silver, and vessels of gold,
and vessels of brass:

Which also king David did dedicate unto the LORD, with the silver and gold that he had dedicated of all nations which he subdued; Of Syria, and of Moab, and of the children of Ammon, and of the Philistines, and of Amalek, and of the spoil of Hadadezer, son of Rehob, king of Zobah. And David gat him a name when he returned from smiting of the Syrians in the valley of salt, being eighteen thousand men.
And he put garrisons in Edom; throughout all Edom put he garrisons, and all they of Edom became David's servants. And the LORD preserved David whithersoever he went. And David reigned over all Israel; and David executed judgment and justice unto all his people. And Joab the son of Zeruiah was over the host; and Jehoshaphat the son of Ahilud was recorder;
2 Samuel 8:8-16 (KJV)

Yet in this book in which we do not read the Word 'God', we find God's unusual intervention, because the One who keeps Israel neither slumbers nor sleeps.

Behold, he that keepeth Israel shall neither slumber nor sleep.
Psalms 121:4 (KJV)

Whoever you are who is reading this book, it is time for your divine vindication. A God who could turn this situation that seemed concluded around and give His people unusual victory would

104

turn yours around too. It is time for you to receive all that God has earmarked for you; a thousand Hamans will not be able to stop you. The windows of God's favour will be open to you. Difficult people and situations will have to change, because God's hand is upon your life.

Get ready for your coming breakthrough that would arrive suddenly.

> And David came to Baalperazim, and David smote them there, and said, The LORD hath broken forth upon mine enemies before me, as the breach of waters. Therefore he called the name of that place Baalperazim.
> 2 Samuel 5:20 (KJV)

Deliverance must come for you in Zion.

> And it shall come to pass, that whosoever shall call on the name of the LORD shall be delivered: for in mount Zion and in Jerusalem shall be deliverance, as the LORD hath said, and in the remnant whom the LORD shall call.
> Joel 2:32 (KJV)

You will overcome and enter into the fullness of your favour. What was called problems will introduce you to the testimony God meant for you to have. Every family problem will experience solution. Solution will follow impossible situations, solution will follow your family challenges, and solution will follow your financial challenges.

Everything and everyone that made itself an opposition to you becomes an opposition to God, so it is time for your victory. Every stronghold of the enemy will bow to the name of the Lord in your mouth. This is your day to walk in victory, refuse to settle for less.

In 24 hours, this anointing changed the course of history for the Jews and lifted a poor man and made him to share tables with the princes of this world. Yours will not be an exception. Every spirit that calls itself your enemy will suffer disastrous defeat.

Welcome to the world of the 24 hour breakthrough. Enter through the gate of abundance. Begin the journey of accomplishment, because failure is over.

Engage your mind for uncommon joy; uncommon pleasure in God, the one who brought you this far is changing your story totally.

The case of Esther can be compared to a game of chess, God and satan are the invisible players moving kings and queens for their purposes. When satan knocked out many other people and put Haman in place, he thought the game was over. At least from the boast of Haman, he must have thought "Check mate", unknown to him that our King still has one more move. One more move of victory, one more move of testimony.

So when Haman was busy announcing "Check mate", there usually, once in a while in the game of chess, the queen being the chief mover maybe sacrificed for the king who having made one previous move can only make one more move. When Esther said, as if she knew she had to be sacrificed, "If I perish, I perish".

So with the queen of this earth out of the way, the King of the Universe took charge. He had to make one more move to bring the final victory, so Haman who thought it was over, discovered until God makes it over, it is not over.

Whenever satan comes with all ferocity, just remember the King has one more move:

*To get you out of broke to blessed, the King has one more move.

*To take you from sickness to health, the King has one more move.

*To take you from loss to gain, the King has one more move.

*To take you from suffering to enjoyment, the King has one more move.

*To take you from being the possessed to become the possessor of blessings, the King has one more move.

*To take you from being the chained to take you to freedom, the King has one more move.

*To take you from crying to laughing, the King has one more move.

*To change you from barrenness to fruitfulness, the King has one more move.

*To take you from curses to blessing, the King has one more move.

*To move you from hell to heavenly places, the King has one more move.

So He allowed the battle, He fought it for us, He delivered the breakthrough. Every 24 hour miracle is preceded by a battle or a process you may have to go through. In such battles you may be troubled on every side, the result though is that God's plan for your life becomes manifest and so it is not the time to let go or release your destiny to facts, fate, faces or fear.

We are hedged in (pressed) on every side [troubled and oppressed in every way], but not cramped or crushed; we suffer embarrassments and are perplexed and unable to find a way out, but not driven to despair; We are pursued (persecuted and hard driven), but not deserted [to stand alone]; we are struck down to the ground, but never struck out and destroyed; Always carrying about in the body the liability and exposure to the same putting to death that the Lord Jesus suffered, so that the [resurrection] life of Jesus also may be shown forth by and in our bodies.

2 Corinthians 4:8-10 (Amplified)

# CHAPTER 4

# MEPHIBOSETH

## From rejection to restoration

The world will try to crucify you personally if you do not know how to watch and refuse to let it. People are never satisfied with whom God has made us to be. It is as if the industry that wants to convert everyone and make them something else thrives forever. People who are short are made to feel that they have to be tall. Those who are tall want to become short; people who are lighter want to become darker. The educated act as if they want to be lesser educated, the lesser-educated want to be more educated. The quest for change is ever persistent.

Not only will people try to define you, they will also try to classify you and if you can be classified, then you can be nullified. If you can be classified the world can re-define you. Such persistent attempts by people to make us who we are not or who they want us to be, never stops because we become born-again. It is in our hand to choose to not allow people to determine who we become. The ability to not allow yourself to be made what people want, only finds its true depth and anchor in your self-knowledge in Christ Jesus. That is you knowing who you are in the Lord.

Among whom also we all had our conversation in times past in the lusts of our flesh, fulfilling the desires of the flesh and of the mind; and were by nature the children of wrath, even as others.
Ephesians 2:3 (KJV)

And hath raised us up together, and made us sit together in heavenly places in Christ Jesus:
Ephesians 2:6 (KJV)

Once you are aware and are able to establish your divine connection, your understanding helps you live a life that transcends colour, societal stature or natural connection. Such knowledge helps you reach a point where, the weakness or strength of the home you come from no longer makes any impact. It is into such a world that Mephiboseth found himself.

A man born into royalty, destined to inherit the throne, to rule along with his grandfather and father, but for whom the fortunes turned. His parents destroyed, his father killed in battle, his nurse dropping him on the way to Lodebar as she ran away from the raging army of Joab, who were looking for every member of the house of Saul to kill. His nurse took him to Lodebar, an empty place without pasture, where the chance of survival was very slim.

Yet it is from this story, that of this crippled Mephiboseth that we see the manifestation of the 24-hour miracle. The intervention of God in spite of situations, to within a short time moved people from the mess they are in, to 'the message' they should be. In the case of Mephiboseth, from utter rejection to total restoration.

Firstly though let us see the catalogue of troubles this young prince faced.

# THE CATALOGUE OF TROUBLES

On Mount Gilboa, King Saul and Prince Jonathan, his grandfather and father, fought the army of the Philistines until Israel was outmatched and under-equipped, as they were routed by the Philistines. Such defeat meant a weakened nation and a weakened royalty. Ishboseth, another son of King Saul ruled for a short while before David's army routed everyone of the household of Saul. They all died, except for Mephiboseth who, the nurse on the run had served as the source of his protection.

Mephiboseth this young prince, the grandson of a king, did not claim his royalty or inheritance, at least not anytime, possibly because, as his name would reveal he was too ashamed to even be part of his royal connection. You might say he allowed his circumstance to determine who he would become, exchanging the truths of his position, with a lie of his situation. Mephiboseth must have accepted his perpetual change to failure and degradation, his constant acquaintance with tragedy and catalogue of trouble.

# A MAN CALLED SHAME

The name 'Mephiboseth' simply broken down comes from the Hebrew word 'bosh' which means shame, 'boseth' which means shameful. While 'Mephi-boseth' takes it to another level to make it mean "One who distributes shame". A close look at Mephiboseth's life shows that:

## 1.    He lived in fear

Fear has a way of binding people. Fear makes a big thing out of a small thing. Fear made the memory of his royalty fade away with the reality of his temporal situation more clearly in his mind. Fear made the memory of his father's valour and his grandfather's victory to possibly be nothing to Mephiboseth. The fear of being taunted by friends and children he knew when he grew, the fear of being looked at as one without legs. The fears of the handicapped boy who could not rise to the prowess of his fathers made him to stay in doors. He possibly imagined how people would kill him, if he ever stayed to declare whose son he was.

Fear has torment, always remember God has not given you the spirit of fear.

> For God hath not given us the spirit of fear; but of power, and of love, and of a sound mind.
> 2 Timothy 1:7 (KJV)

It is an instrument of satan to put you in perpetual bondage.

## 2.    He believed in a lie

When fear paints a picture, it is not yet a tragedy until you believe in it.  Fear takes advantage of your power of imagination and the enemy turns it around to sell satan's lies.  Lies come from the pit of hell, with satan being the father of it.

> Ye are of your father the devil, and the lusts of your father ye will do. He was a murderer from the beginning, and abode not in the truth, because there is no truth in him. When he speaketh a lie, he speaketh of his own: for he is a liar, and the father of it.
> John 8:44 (KJV)

Mephiboseth believed the lie told to him by the devil about his condition.  He believed a lie about his grandfather's mistakes and allowed them to hold him down from becoming whom God said he is.  Many people run away from the Lord because they believe a lie.  Many people run away from realities of whom God wants to make them, because they believe a lie.  Satan knows how to tell a lie that they will not succeed; he knows how to tell a lie that you will not overcome.  Whereas, satan's lies cannot erase what God has set in motion.

Nay, in all these things we are more than conquerors
through him that loved us.
Romans 8:37 (KJV)

It is a lie that sin will have dominion over you. The
Scriptures say the reverse.

For sin shall not have dominion over you: for ye are
not under the law, but under grace.
Romans 6:14 (KJV)

Sometimes people hide behind these lies of satan and
refuse to attempt to be whom God wants them to be.
Experiences of the past can be used to attack your mind.

An abusive relationship you have known in the past, a
mental lapse you have once experienced.
An un-confessed dark sin that still plagues your mind.
A sinful past you are afraid might be discovered.
An emotional hurt that holds you down.

Mephiboseth felt intimidated, he succumbed to the fear
of men, then to the fear of God. He was intimidated by
his physical handicap and what men might think of him.
He held onto his rags and hid himself in the dark little
hut which his father's servant Ziba must have provided
for him.

Like Mephiboseth, we sometimes accept the crutches of
humiliation. We refuse to stand firm on what God thinks
of us. We are perpetually and particularly worried of
what men think of us.

In God have I put my trust: I will not be afraid what
man can do unto me.
Psalms 56:11 (KJV)

Having endured the ridicule of his upbringing, he felt
intimidated by the fact that he was put down all his life,
having been dropped by his nurse.

## THE NURSE WHO DROPPED HIM

Mephiboseth's name reveals 'the shameful one'. A man
who, as his nurse ran from the approaching soldiers fell
and dropped him, thus damaging the young prince. Being
dropped has an impact it leaves on ones life.

Dropped people always feel broken.

Dropped people always shameful.

Dropped people always feel inadequate.

Dropped people always feel troubled.

Dropped people are often oversensitive
about even the smallest of matters.

Dropped people become secretive, even if
they have no secrets to hide.

The dropping permanently crippled
Mephiboseth, he was not only physically
crippled, he was also emotionally crippled.

Emotionally crippled people do not know how to give love.

They sometimes know they have a problem, but yet feel perpetually unable to break out of this inability. Emotionally crippled people suspect, givers of love. They often feel that it is not genuine. Emotionally crippled people feel every positive thing that comes their way must be fraudulent and therefore is to be suspected. They think also that they have to buy love and are perpetually into the habit of trying to please people.

He must have also been spiritually crippled. We have no account of his relationship with God or desire to serve the Lord. We have no recollection in Scripture of him seeking God's touch, yet the Scripture says there is a balm in Gilead to make even the worse person whole.

Is there no balm in Gilead; is there no physician there? why then is not the health of the daughter of my people recovered?
Jeremiah 8:22 (KJV)

## HE LIVED IN A PLACE CALLED EMPTY

Lodebar, an evil, geographical terrain. Lodebar, a place that means 'empty, pastureless, no communication'. As the nurse took Mephiboseth and ran from the army, she went on for three days until she came to Lodebar, one of the most deserted places on earth. So impoverished, you would hardly believe anyone lives there. It certainly was not a place fit for raising a man who should one day rule Israel. Lodebar, a place so depressing, it seems like God has forsaken every inch of it. The winds blew the dry grass and the few houses there were covered in dust. Nobody goes to Lodebar. A few pilgrims may have stopped once in a while, but there certainly was nothing of historical significance ever recorded about Lodebar.

It is a place symbolic of spiritual bondage, loneliness, hardship and pain. This is where Mephiboseth found himself, a depressing place that held no future for anyone. Geography matters, because where you live determines who you become. It affects who you see, it determines who sees you. Where you live shapes you, it affects your perspective on life. Psychologists say we are products not only of our genetic inheritance, but also the environment of our upbringing. Where you live can affect and determine your destiny.

Certainly Lodebar only held Mephiboseth down. How many people have also found themselves held down by memories of places where they were once raised; where they once lived and never made progress.

# THE NEIGHBOUR CALLED 'SELL OUT'

Every detail of Mephiboseth's upbringing and life gives us a picture of what things were like. He was said to live in this broken down, almost God-forsaken village called 'empty' in the house of Machir. Machir's name means 'Sold out'. It is also a mirror of what people like Mephiboseth do. They sell out to situations, they sell out to the challenges of life. Mephiboseth sold out to his circumstance. Possibly the enemy told him his circumstance could not change, he has to accept things the way they are and say that is what life has apportioned to him.

Satan tries to tell you that you are 'under' the circumstance. "Under the circumstance in which you are, there is little you can do." God has not called you to be under the circumstance; you are head and not tail, above and not beneath. Your circumstance should not dictate your focus, because you should not live under the circumstance. The word circumstance comes from two Latin words, 'circum' 'stance'. The 'circle of standing'. Whenever people feel boxed in within a circle, they think they cannot come out of the circle and have to accept whatever life dishes to them within the circle. So they sell out to the situation.

The Word of God should dictate your future and not 'Machir', the place of 'Sell outs'. When you live in Machir:

You give up your palace for a pit
You give up your position for pennies
You give up your birthright for bread
You give up your calling for crumbs
You give up your purity for pleasure

How he got here must have been a combination of the effort of the nurse who dropped him and the grumpy old servant.:

## THE GRUMPY OLD SERVANT

Mephiboseth found himself in the company of Ziba, an aged servant who once served the Lord's Anointed, King Saul and now has to serve a crippled child. Ziba, a man who once knew privilege, even though he served. He entertained kings and queens, priests and priestesses. He announced the arrival of Diplomats in the palace of King Saul. He was the first to see distinguished men from distant lands that came to see the king, but now he had to hang around a crippled child.

Ziba possibly remembered the good old days, but yet has found himself attached to a broken man. It is sad when we find ourselves beside men like Mephiboseth and all we think of or see is the trouble they are in. We fail to realise that our destiny and future may be attached to such men.

Following the coronation of David, Ziba must have

hidden himself somewhere on the outskirts of Jerusalem. Afraid to be caught and identified with his former boss, his future had been impoverished; his existence had been a difficult one.

# THE CALL FROM THE PALACE

A day comes when salvation comes to any man. The 24 hour miracle about which this book is starts with an act of God. An act that could not have been thought to be possible where it to be in the analysis of men.

And there was of the house of Saul a servant whose name was Ziba. And when they had called him unto David, the king said unto him, Art thou Ziba? And he said, Thy servant is he. And the king said, Is there not yet any of the house of Saul, that I may shew the kindness of God unto him? And Ziba said unto the king, Jonathan hath yet a son, which is lame on his feet.
2 Samuel 9:2-3 (KJV)

The king had chosen to remember the need to bless someone from the house of Jonathan. In spite of the brokenness of Mephiboseth and his apparent hopelessness in the situation in which he was, God was about to move on his behalf. The stone the builders rejected is about to become the chief cornerstone. The 24 hour anointing is stirring up, God is beginning a move, "which the devil can't stop, can't stand and can do nothing about".

The God who owns the heart of kings was now stirring the one who he called 'His beloved'.

The king's heart is in the hand of the LORD, as the rivers of water: he turneth it whithersoever he will.
Proverbs 21:1 (KJV)

For the king announces to everyone, "Is there anyone of the house of Saul that I may show the kindness of God. David's questions were motivated by relationships. May God send you people who in your moment of need will be connected to you, not by the things you will be able to give them, but the calling upon their life to be able to relate to you. People who are instruments of healing, people who are instruments of hope to you. Relationships matter, who you run with matters, certain people are not sent to be in your life. Every man has their exit point when they are not meant to be with you.

There are people who are not sent to be in your life. Those who distract you, those who divide your attention, those who destroy your testimony, those who devalue your person, they are not sent to be in your journey. You must recognise them and put them where they belong. It took only one Jonah to sink a boat, it also took only one Jesus to keep a boat floating. Every stranger in your boat whom God has not sent to be in your journey, it is my prayer that they will be exposed and expelled.

The King was seeking a long forgotten orphan, to raise to a place of elegance and beauty because of relationship. Even Jesus had levels of relationship. He never spoke on the same manner with the multitude as He did with the twelve apostles. David was also committed to the covenant of love and kindness, we read, "For Jonathan's sake". The Scripture would say.

> Greater love hath no man than this, that a man lay down his life for his friends.
> John 15:13 (KJV)

This covenant of love carries with it the power of protection. When ancient ones went into covenant they were committed to each other and to each other's family. To extend the hand of protection and never harm those with whom they relate, to a third and fourth generation. David's commitment was irrespective of Mephiboseth's condition. Covenant had more power than the physical ability of the recipient to reciprocate.

It was irrespective of Mehiboseth's residence. Covenant has more power than the place the recipient lived. It was irrespective of Mephiboseth's many challenges in life.

When favour and grace breaks upon your life, when your season to be blessed comes, the challenges you have cannot stop it.

> Thou shalt arise, and have mercy upon Zion: for the
> time to favour her, yea, the set time, is come.
> Psalms 102:13 (KJV)

The smell around Mephiboseth cannot stop the favour about to break on him. The dark, dinky room in which he lived, the few clay pots with which he ate, the utensils he used for his meal, the dirty hut, the smelly clothes, the unshaved beard, the uncut hair, the unwashed body cannot stop what covenant had put in motion.

> But as it is written, Eye hath not seen, nor ear heard,
> neither have entered into the heart of man, the things
> which God hath prepared for them that love him.
> 1 Corinthians 2:9 (KJV)

He may have been a deposed, dejected royal, yet God was about to turn the situation around because of covenant.

> When a man's ways please the LORD, he maketh even
> his enemies to be at peace with him.
> Proverbs 16:7 (KJV)

# THE 24 HOUR MIRACLE

Within 24-hours the royal chariots were rolled out. Ziba confirms he knows where Mephiboseth is; the king gave a word before his army. Mephiboseth must be fetched because his time for a change has come. In that one day, Lodebar was about to receive a royal visit. A place of emptiness, the house of a sell out was about to experience a visit from the palace of the king to pick a man whose name was shame. A man whom within 24-hours would come into a new season.

It is hard to tell what happened on the day, as the soldiers arrived in this frontier to pick Mephiboseth. It is certain as he looked back as the chariots sped away that he must have said, "I am not coming back". For those who read this book today, it is important to look back at your Lodebar, the place of your emptiness, and say, "I am not coming back". It is important to look at the place of your sell-out and say, "I am not coming back". For those who read this book today, it is important to look back at your Lodebar, the place of your emptiness, and say, "I am not coming back". It is important to look at the place of your sell-out and say, "I am not coming back". You need to say goodbye to the place where all you have known is shame and embarrassment.

Within 24 hours Mephiboseth would very soon find himself in the great palace of King David Ben Jesse. Ushered quickly into the royal bath where he would take his wash for the first time after a long time. Certainly not an ordinary one, as royals were known to wash with the best perfumes available and the softest of soaps. Dressed as royal, ready to meet the king, all within 24 hours.

As Mephiboseth appeared before David, the king embraced him and in those few hours brought him into:

## 1.    A Reassurance

And David said unto him, Fear not: for I will surely shew thee kindness for Jonathan thy father's sake, and will restore thee all the land of Saul thy father; and thou shalt eat bread at my table continually.
2 Samuel 9:7 (KJV)

The sentence of death pronounced upon Mephiboseth was from this moment broken. The one who was once hiding all those years suddenly hears the announcement that the royal highness requests his presence and upon his appearance before the king, we find that his disgrace has been changed by God's grace and he was reassured that he had nothing to fear. The power fear had over him was broken at this moment.

## 2.    Restoration

...... and will restore thee all the land of Saul thy father;
and thou shalt eat bread at my table continually.
2 Samuel 9:7 (KJV)

He never owned anything, the food he ate was at the
mercy of Ziba who had to bring it three days journey.
The clothes he wore were at the mercy of people who
passed on and handed down their second-hand clothes.
But today the boy who never owned anything but rags
was suddenly going to own the land that belonged to
kings.

There is a favour that is coming in these last
days upon believers, by reason of a 24 hour
miracle, it will be such that you did not work
for it, labour for it, but it has been put in
place for you.    Uncommon blessing, uncommon
breakthrough.  The ones you did not know are coming
your way.

But as it is written, Eye hath not seen, nor ear heard,
neither have entered into the heart of man, the things
which God hath prepared for them that love him.
1 Corinthians 2:9 (KJV)

That which the palmerworm hath left hath the locust
eaten; and that which the locust hath left hath the

cankerworm eaten; and that which the cankerworm hath
left hath the caterpiller eaten.

Joel 1:4 (KJV)

In 24 hours the man who had no leg to walk and lived in a village that was not on the map. In the house of a man who was a sell out and all his life was called a shame now was given the land that was only fit for kings.

God is going to bring you into your own seasons of restoration, when the things you thought you lost will be given to you as a man who has been blessed and highly favoured.

## 3.    Regards

His name was always called shame; people could walk past him and take him for another vagrant who crawled on his backside. His life was dependent on the goodwill of servants, but today God has regard for him.

Then said Ziba unto the king, According to all that my lord the king hath commanded his servant, so shall thy servant do. As for Mephibosheth, said the king, he shall eat at my table, as one of the king's sons.

2 Samuel 9:11 (KJV)

The king has made an announcement, "He shall eat at my table as one of the king's son." He had not washed probably for many years but today God was restoring a lost glory and dignity.

For thou hast been a shelter for me, and a strong tower from the enemy.
Psalms 61:3 (KJV)

When God decides to bring colour into your life and give you dignity where you never knew it, nobody can stop it.

## 4.     Royalty

Then the king called to Ziba, Saul's servant, and said unto him, I have given unto thy master's son all that pertained to Saul and to all his house. Thou therefore, and thy sons, and thy servants, shall till the land for him, and thou shalt bring in the fruits, that thy master's son may have food to eat: but Mephibosheth thy master's son shall eat bread alway at my table. Now Ziba had fifteen sons and twenty servants.
2 Samuel 9:9-10 (KJV)

By birth he was royalty, by upbringing he never enjoyed it. He knew poverty and was acquainted with it, yet in 24 hours, the anointing that destroys yokes and removes burdens also restores what you may have lost, raised him to the seat he never thought he could have.

Among whom also we all had our conversation in times past in the lusts of our flesh, fulfilling the desires of the flesh and of the mind; and were by nature the children of wrath, even as others.
Ephesians 2:3 (KJV)

And hath raised us up together, and made us sit together in heavenly places in Christ Jesus:
Ephesians 2:6 (KJV)

He raiseth up the poor out of the dust, and lifteth up the beggar from the dunghill, to set them among princes, and to make them inherit the throne of glory: for the pillars of the earth are the LORD'S, and he hath set the world upon them.
1 Samuel 2:8 (KJV)

Today God has raised Mephiboseth to sit with the princes of the land and as long as he is seated with them, the eyes of men will not be on his weakness but on the position he occupies. No more will he drag on the streets of Lodebar, he has been elevated. He has been put in a position men thought he could never have.

For promotion cometh neither from the east, nor from the west, nor from the south.
Psalms 75:6 (KJV)

His eyes had grown accustomed to pain, but today the story changes. He had probably said, "I will never amount to anything, but a reject, a cast off." Yet today the story has changed. Among the princes of the palace of David is the man they have to call Prince Mephiboseth.

His only claim to fame used to be, "My grandfather used to be, my father used to be", but today he can safely say that by reason of a 24 hour anointing, "I am who I am in God".

He worked hard to eat from broken plates, but today he has a dinner date with the king. The feeble legs that made him unqualified have now become God's instrument for lifting him up. What satan calls a man's weakness can become the stepping-stone to take him to the next level. For where we are fought the most becomes where we are known the most to experience the grace and victory of God.

People who read this book today, may have been pained by what they experienced, but God knows how to bring beauty out of one's ashes. Just as a helpless cripple found compassion from a magnanimous king, may help come for you from above.

I was glad when they said unto me, Let us go into the house of the LORD.
Psalms 122:1 (KJV)

People in high places will run helter-skelter to make things happen for you. So we see as God would give Mephiboseth regard, it was King David himself who met him and caused him to sit in a place that would be his testimony.

## 5. Riches

What do you do if all you have known is brokenness and poverty and suddenly wealth and blessing is thrust into your hands? Certainly for a man like Mephiboseth, it could not change him. It is those who have died to certain things that are not easily changed by it when it comes into their hands.

> And David said unto him, Fear not: for I will surely shew thee kindness for Jonathan thy father's sake, and will restore thee all the land of Saul thy father; and thou shalt eat bread at my table continually.
>
> 2 Samuel 9:7 (KJV)

> Then the king called to Ziba, Saul's servant, and said unto him, I have given unto thy master's son all that pertained to Saul and to all his house. Thou therefore, and thy sons, and thy servants, shall till the land for him, and thou shalt bring in the fruits, that thy master's son may have food to eat: but Mephibosheth thy master's son shall eat bread alway at my table. Now Ziba had fifteen sons and twenty servants. Then said Ziba unto the king, According to all that my lord the king hath com-

manded his servant, so shall thy servant do. As for
Mephibosheth, said the king, he shall eat at my table, as
one of the king's sons. And Mephibosheth had a young
son, whose name was Micha. And all that dwelt in the
house of Ziba were servants unto Mephibosheth.

2 Samuel 9:9-12 (KJV)

God never gives any man ten talents until he qualifies for
the first, then two talents, then five talents and then He
promotes to ten talents. The times Mephiboseth when
through his test with God we do not know, but today is
his day of promotion to receive his ten talents. Yes his
eyes had grown accustomed to lack, but today is his day
of provision.

Poverty has a way of shaping your mind-set;
it makes you think that any manner of blessing should be suspected. Emptiness has a
way of making you feel full. What an oxy-
moron. Empty, yet feeling full. The splendour of
kings looks like a wasted opulence because when you
have known empty, you think that all you have known is
what life is.

Today he has been brought into favour, uncommon
favour, so that he can turn around and use it to bless others. May God bring you my reader into an uncommon
blessing.

For ye know the grace of our Lord Jesus Christ, that,
though he was rich, yet for your sakes he became poor,
that ye through his poverty might be rich.
2 Corinthians 8:9 (KJV)

And God is able to make all grace abound toward you;
that ye, always having all sufficiency in all things, may
abound to every good work:
2 Corinthians 9:8 (KJV)

Mephiboseth is far from the ideal person to receive
wealth, abundance and favour. He did not look qualified;
he did not talk like he was qualified. Yes he had some
royal blood but nothing of his upbringing, placement or
life reflected the blood that flowed through his vein. God
did not give him the blessing because he was royalty; it
was a favour he never deserved. Get ready for God to
give you an abundance of His favour, the showers of his
blessing.

And I will make them and the places round about my
hill a blessing; and I will cause the shower to come
down in his season; there shall be showers of blessing.
Ezekiel 34:26 (KJV)

Mephiboseth came clutching rags, but today he is staying
in the palace because favour has a way, in the 24-hour
experience of bringing you into a position that is not
imaginable, by bringing you into a lifting that could not
have happened by human effort.

In conclusion I challenge you today, that there is a 24 hour anointing breaking upon your life. You may have not seen much hitherto, but God sees great potential. He will lift you up. God sees your future position; He will bring you into it. Some look at you like Mephiboseth and see nobody. They walk past you as if you did not exist; you were just one more number. God who knows how to make somebody out of nobody will yet surprise you and people around you. You were one time not a people, but God has invited to you to sit with the best he has.

Which in time past were not a people, but are now the people of God: which had not obtained mercy, but now have obtained mercy.
1 Peter 2:10 (KJV)

As long as they look at where you are now seated, your past is irrelevant. That is how you are called to be and by reason of a 24-hour anointing, it makes manifest the promises that are in Christ Jesus, which are yea and Amen.

For all the promises of God in him are yea, and in him Amen, unto the glory of God by us.
2 Corinthians 1:20 (KJV)

God has pre-destined you to enjoy all that He has. You will not miss a little of it. Like Mephiboseth, when your 24 hour miracle breaks forth, it may not be now, it may not be in a week, it may not be this month but keep on expecting that. It certainly when it breaks forth there will be such radical changes. God will shatter the backbone of lack in your life.

The old lion perisheth for lack of prey, and the stout lion's whelps are scattered abroad.
Job 4:11 (KJV)

He will destroy the power of scarcity.

But my God shall supply all your need according to his riches in glory by Christ Jesus.
Philippians 4:19 (KJV)

God will bring you into superabundance.

Therefore, my beloved brethren, be ye stedfast, unmoveable, always abounding in the work of the Lord, forasmuch as ye know that your labour is not in vain in the Lord.
1 Corinthians 15:58 (KJV)

God will disappoint the spirit that is releasing crumbs to your life. You will go from crumbs to feasting.

Behold, the days come, saith the LORD, that the plowman shall overtake the reaper, and the treader of grapes him that soweth seed; and the mountains shall drop sweet wine, and all the hills shall melt.
Amos 9:13 (KJV)

You will go from penury into inheritance.

And every man that striveth for the mastery is
temperate in all things. Now they do it to obtain a
corruptible crown; but we an incorruptible.
1 Corinthians 9:25 (KJV)

Every stolen property from you that was stolen by the
tragedies you have experienced, the emptiness, the sell
out, the shame will turn around to a seven-fold restoration.

That which the palmerworm hath left hath the locust
eaten; and that which the locust hath left hath the
cankerworm eaten; and that which the cankerworm hath
left hath the caterpiller eaten.
Joel 1:4 (KJV)

Every evil attraction you had stops from today. Your
Lodebar, your place of emptiness, your place
of dry pastures will turn around to become
the place of your fullness. God will cause you to
yet bear fruit beyond your imagination. The Lord will
bring you into the place of superabundance, the place
where you would only know leftovers and not lack. The
place where you will go from grace to grace, from blessing to blessing, from favour to favour. It is time for a new
change. It is time for the outbreak of the 24 hour anointing.

# TESTIMONIES

Dear Pastor,

Thank God it is a new day in the life of the church. We serve an ever-faithful God. You prayed about the 24 hour miracle on Sunday night 19/08/01, and I believed and eagerly expected God's intervention on a number of things I've been believing him for.

To start with, for about three weeks now, my spirit has been rejoicing concerning IGOC 2001, like a bride awaits her groom with expectation. Thank God the bible says the expectation of the righteous shall not be cut short. I did not have a penny on me to register. On Sunday, I was blessed with £20; I gave £10 offering from it the same night. Came to the conference this morning and was about to pay the conference fee by overdraft when a lady told me to cancel my detail from the form I had filled because she's got a spare pass to give me.

You can imagine my joy because God miraculously provided me with a pass. I know this is just the beginning, more testimonies are on the way because what he has set to do in my life, the devil can't stop it.... and there's nothing he can do about it. It's only two days since the conference started and from all the teachings so far, I've never been more blessed in my life.

Pastor, keep up the good work and by the grace of the living God, I will be part of the company of believers who will continually uphold your hand both financially and spiritually. Amen.

L

Dear Pastor

I have been short listed for a job I had been believing God for. I was at the IGOC meeting on Sunday night. Praise God for he is good. He has been good to my family and I.

SB.

Dear All,

Someone just walked up to the Reception a few minutes ago and asked to see me (without any prior appointment, I didn't even know her name). She said she has been instructed to sow a seed into my life without explaining. So she handed me an 'envelope' and went off home!

My 24 hour miracles have started. I have still got 5 more hours till 9pm!!

AY

Dear Congregation,

As we attended yesterday at the International Gathering of Champions and heard Pastor Mathew and Dr. Mike Murdock speaking about the (our!) 24 hour miracle, God moved in our hearts. So today is the day God will move in our life!

And He has already started... We arrived at our little place yesterday night at about 2:30 am, and as expected we were worn out... Now normally we get up at an early hour and run to our door when the post arrives (okay slightly exaggerated, but still close to reality). Today we slept right through it and as we have just woken up and checked the post God confirmed His intentions:

1.There was a letter in the post for my wife to come and attend a job interview for a post at BBC Three Counties radio. We have been praying and believing that God would provide His job for us and move us further to extend His kingdom. One of the great things about the interview is that it will be held in Cambridge, a place that is on our top three lists to visit, as I am Dutch and have been in the country for just over a year. The BBC has asked my wife to prepare two story ideas to present at local television and/or radio. It is our prayer - and we request you would stand with us - that God will again inspire her to present His idea in a creative and attractive way.

2. I personally am also looking for a new job, and yesterday was a confirmation to my heart. This morning as I opened the post and received a letter confirming my National Insurance Number. At the time Social Security explained it could take up to six months to process my application. Now a month down the line God has opened up a way for it to be processed ready for my next job.

Now these things may seem minor to an outsider, but to us they are a major confirmation of Gods work in our life. They truly are building blocks for our recent marriage - we are married now for almost two months. By the way, God confirmed to my wife that she would meet me at the Gathering '99. We met two months later doing missionary work in Uganda.

God is good and we want to give Him all He deserves - that is our whole life. We believe that by the blood of the Lamb and the words of our testimony the enemy is defeated. Therefore we want to publicly testify of what God is doing in our life!

We will keep you posted throughout the day and look forward to being with you again coming Thursday.
Many blessings,
T & D H

Dear Sir,

I greet you and I salute your heart that was full of love and passion according to our Lord JESUS CHRIST has laid it in your spirit. Sir, the work that GOD has assigned for you to care for the poor and the low life people and you are doing it whole heartedly will be rewarded in the mighty name of JESUS. KICC will continue to grow more and more in the mighty name of JESUS. Rev Matthew Ashimolowo and all the church workers are specially anointed for the work of GOD.

I always pray to be part of this. I believe my prayers will be answered soon. All my life, I have never being lucky to see face to face good preachers that encourages, praying, anointing, wanting people to reach maximum level in life. But just for attending the church alone my life has changed a lot, everything that owns me is JESUS, JESUS, JESUS, is so hard to explain. When I sleep, when I am alone, in the bathroom, etc. I will be talking to myself, praying at all time, read the Bible and study it, Total transformation. I seek for JESUS with all my heart, and I found him, JESUS showed up to me face to face in my dream, it was the most scary day of my life. It is another encounter completely, sir believe it or not JESUS said to me that HE IS COMING BACK SOON, and we should engage ourselves in salvation of people's souls rather than anything else. I printed leaflets, tracts and wrote everything he told me in it and distributed them in to houses, just according to the direction I received from my dream. Why I am saying this, is to let you know the anointing of GOD I have now since I started attending KICC.

Secondly, I was in the church yesterday for service and I prayed for a 24hour miracle. This morning, I received a letter from a place of work where I was told that my application is successful. I was really happy, even though I have not got the confirmation but I claim it straight away, and I believe that I have got the job. Further testimony will be given as soon as I get the confirmation. May the grace of GOD almighty continue to be with you, your family, co-pastors and all the church workers (amen).
MS


Dear Pastor Matthew,
We would like to thank you and let you know of some of the evidences that the word of God is true in your mouth and ministry.

We had believed God for a breakthrough new job for my wife since November 2000. She had written a myriad of applications and attended various interviews which seemed not to come through with the desired position. In some cases she was told that she was either over or under qualified for the positions she wanted. In one instance she was told she was too ambitious as she was studying to improve her career skills.

On Saturday the 9th of February after the powerful all-night prayer meeting we got home to find a letter of invitation to a job interview for which we had been believing God for. Last Sunday night, you ministered on the 24 hour Miracle and we held on to the word with all our hearts. When Pastor Yemisi came to bless the offerings she also said that by the next day, as the office opened there would be a lot of testimonies waiting. We clung unto that word also.

The very next day my wife went for the interview and she was the last candidate to be seen for the job. During her interview she saw the grades awarded to each candidate for their application forms. Her mark of 7/10 was the lowest while some candidates had as high 9.5/10. Even though seeing these grades was an error on the part of her interviewers, she confessed the word that said, "The last shall be the first". Of course, you guessed right! Just as the office opened on Tuesday she had a telephone call confirming that she had got the job! This was a 25% increase in her previous salary, contrary to the opinion of her employment agents.

God has really been faithful. A few months ago we bought our first property by God's divine intervention. I started my PhD studentship and I have had such accelerated breakthroughs in my research work, that very soon I would be publishing the first of many papers in the field.

We just want to appreciate you and your wife. We shall be back shortly with many more testimonies.

God bless real good.
O & T O


Dear Pastor Matthew,

I am writing in my testimony in regards to my 24 hour miracle. In fact, I have two different testimonies that happened within 24 hours. On Monday morning, I came in to work as usual expecting nothing different. My manager called me into her office and from the stern look on her face I really thought I had done something wrong. When I got to her office she smiled broadly and said she had received confirmation from the head of our department to give me a pay rise, backdating it as well. That was not all, she said I would receive another pay raise in April when the new financial year begun!!! I just can't stop thanking God for his faithfulness especially due to the fact that lately finances have been a bit tight and I have been a bit worried. Sometimes it is in the areas we least expect that God meets us at our point of need. I never expected God to work this way. It is indeed "the Lord's doing and it is marvellous in my eyes."

That same evening I got home and decided to search for my driving licence again. I had been searching for it for a few weeks and had begun to get anxious, as I needed to produce it very soon as identification. I had even tried to get a duplicate and was informed that I needed to send certain documents which I do not currently have in my possession. A friend had even offered to get one for me through dodgy means if I would pay an exorbitant fee.!!! I knew that this way would not glory God and I would never be able to give this testimony in the congregation of the righteous. I got home that evening and thanked God for that morning's 24 hour breakthrough and committed this issue also into God's hands. I remembered that you kept saying on Sunday that God would give us that 24 hour breakthrough without any help from us. I began looking through documents that I had already meticulously looked through previously and there was my licence, just lying there. I know that God must have sent his angels to place it there or must have opened my eyes to see but whichever way he chose, he did it for me.

The awesomeness that God would do two 24 hour miracles for me in one day was just too much for me. I started singing, praying and crying all at the same time at the goodness of God to me.

I really thank God for his Word in your mouth, his prophet. Pastor Matthew, I just thank God for your life and his hand over your life. I thank God for bringing us to KICC and placing us under your spiritual leadership where we have thrived and grown. Your selfless desire to see the church prosper and grow spiritually and physically never ceases to amaze me. This joy is always evident on your face when you are giving us someone's testimony. I know that through you, KICC will be a household name reaching the unsaved worldwide for Christ.

Congratulations on your nomination to be a part of the Queen's golden jubilee!

God bless you and your family in Jesus name.
SO

I would like to make this brief and straight to the point. We were in the process of exchanging contracts for the new house God gave us and all of a sudden, our solicitor phones the bank just to confirm the funds and is told the mortgage had been cancelled. I was definitely upset, but at the same time had peace. The song "Hosanna, Hosanna, Hosanna, Hosanna" just found its way in my mouth. I called my wife and told her and at the same time, though disappointed, Be magnified came into her mouth.

We had told family and close friends we would be moving and had made certain arrangements. Wow, what next? While we started to make a plan B, we decided it was time to claim the benefit of the 24 hour miracle. We stood together in prayer, thanking God for the property, for favour etc, went to bed and in the morning, I told my wife it was well. My phone was off at work, but at my break time, I went to check my messages, 2 messages [the number of agreement]. One from my wife and one from the Bank. The Bank said they may have good news for me in about an hour from the time I picked up the message. I called back at about the time and was told there had been some procedural mistake and that the mortgage would be re-offered and my solicitors should get that today. We confirmed this by checking on my mortgage enquirer on the Halifax website.

You may be wandering why this testimony. We had just shared with as many people how the present owners of our shared ownership do not normally buy back the share we own, but by divine interference, what they ordinarily would not do, they did.

The house is a 3 bedroom semi terraced in a good and quiet area with a conservatory, new kitchen, alarm system and can, big garden, garage, is a corner piece and can you beat it has two CCTV cameras for whatever reason.

The word indeed works and we thank God that I am in KICC, at a time like this, we would not be elsewhere!!!

Shalom.
B & Y C


Dear Pastor Matthew,
Thank God for your life and the anointing of God on your life. Since I started attending KICC in 1995, my life has never remained the same. I have grown and learnt to pray and know who I am in Christ and the power of

positive of positive prayer.

Your recent word from God is what my testimony is about. The day you mentioned 24 hour miracle I stood up quickly and grabbed it into my spirit. Pastor, it was like you called my name and I answered.

God spoke to me to start applying for a Deputy Headteacher's job prior to that and I obeyed. So that when you spoke the words for promotion in 24 hours it was in line with what God was speaking to me as well. My house fellowship leader and fellowship members are God sent too. They prayed and agreed with me step by step all the way.

Tuesday 26th of February was the interview for the primary school that I had been short-listed for. The interview was from 10.15 am to 3.00 pm I waited on the Lord on Monday so I can eat on the day of the interview and have strength to last throughout all the rigorous interview tasks and processes. On the morning of the interview I parked outside the gates of the beautiful, modern, new primary school and desired it even more. I then said "God the anointing upon Pastor Matthew's life for promotion and progress, I claim it now. That same anointing for excellence, favour Lord let it be upon me now. Father I claim this school and this job right now." The interview was successful, God gave me strategies to help me win over my competitor and I used them and it worked. It could only have been God. We had a tour of the school with governors, written exercises, lesson observation, presentation and finally the interview. God proved Himself awesome.

God has a purpose for my going to the school because the acting Deputy head who is leaving the school is gay and will not look me in the eye or speak to me at all. I have to start work in April with him; he has to hand over to me until he leaves in July. He has not applied for the job for some reasons and is very unhappy. Please thank God for my promotion and remember me in your prayers. Now I have to fulfil my vow as God has done his own part.

PRAISE THE LORD.

Thank you Pastor
MT

Dear Sir/Madam

I felt it very appropriate to share my family's testimony on the 24 hour miracle God has brought to my family.

I am a member of KICC and a real believer in the words that come out of the prophet of God. While Pastor Matthew was preaching on the 24 hour miracle, on that Sunday I was really looking forward. I told God in my mind that I am waiting for my 24 hour miracle present. Half way through the service, my daughter insisted that she wanted to go to the toilet, at that time I was really getting into the message that Pastor Matthew was preaching on the 24 hour miracle. At this time my wife was feeling a bit uncomfortable because she was pregnant and overdue by few days. My daughter unusually insisted that my wife should take her to the toilet. As she was coming back she called me on the mobile which I had left on to vibrate just in case she needed me.

During her pregnancy, I had asked God that I want the delivery to be easy and no funny epidural (pain relieving drugs). As she was coming back from the toilet she called me and I left the service. We drove to Whipps Cross hospital and as she entered the delivery ward. The contractions became very strong and within 30minutes the baby boy was out without any need for painkillers or stitches. The baby weighed over 8 pounds and was breathing and doing well. Thanks be to God almighty who always hears our prayers. What a great 24 hour miracle.

Dear Pastor Matthew

Praise the Lord! This is just to let you know that I received a 24 hour miracle on 18th February. I attended KICC on 17th February and as you preached under the anointing I reached out and believed.

Since March 2001, there was an unresolved financial matter. On Monday morning 18th, I got a cheque in the post - praise God!

Your ministry has impacted my life - May God bless you and continue to use your ministry to help many others in need. I visit KICC and am always blessed when I do.
VW

The 24 hour miracle has hit my company.

At the beginning of the year we set a target of reaching 20% gain for the year on the accounts that we manage.

(You know for yourself that 20% in one year, is unusually high for any mutual fund /PEP/ ISA.)

Well in 24 hours from Wed 6th at 1:30 p.m. to Thursday 7th we made 29% gain on the funds under management!

We achieved all of one year's target in 24 hours!
Who ever heard such a thing? Must be the 24 hour miracle.
ST

To God be the glory for the things He has done. Last year my son was made to take some of his GCSE exams at year 10 and he passed very well. As a result his school recommended him to apply for Gordonstoun College in Scotland which is one of the best and expensive colleges in the country. Prince Charles was a product of this college. As a single parent, I should have said no because I simply did not have the money but I trusted in God and Pastor Matthew is also always preaching about our children attending the best schools in the country and not inner cities schools.

Because my son was under age, I had to go to Scotland with him. When we arrived at the airport, God had arranged everything we needed. The school met us at the airport with a car and they even put us in a hotel for the two days we stayed at no cost to us. We were told that we are the only family the school had ever done this for and every other candidate was responsible for their own trip and accommodation.

When we got back to London, we were so happy at the way we had been treated like royalty, not knowing that God still had more in store for us! The school refunded our airfares by cheque and to top it all, my son gain admission to Gordonstoun College, guess what, WITH A SCHOLARSHIP!! Praise God, I am so grateful to God and my Pastor for making the Word of God practical in our lives. Thank you Lord!!!

I heard about KICC on TV when Pastor Matthew was preaching on the eagle believer back in my country. This February, my family started coming to KICC and was again blessed with the 24 hour miracle sermons. Miracles then stared flowing my way.

1st Miracle: My work involves several difficult tasks, my boss who is a very difficult person called me in within 24 hours to congratulate me on a job well done.

2nd Miracle: The Bible says you have not because you ask not, ask and it shall be given to you. We were trusting the Lord to bless us with a BIG HOME! True to His Word, He blessed us with a big house that's big enough for all our four children and the bonus point is that it is within walking distance to my place of work.

3rd Miracle: My husband and I with our four children had been coming to church by bus, in fact catching four buses to get to church for the service. After the 24 hour miracle sermon, we once again trusted God to ease our transport problem and He surely did. I went to work after the sermon and came home in a fully paid family car!!!! Praise God for my family and myself.

Dear Pastor Matthew

I have a 24 hour miracle. My husband went to the USA on a two years visa and was getting ready to come back home because his visa was not renewed and everyone was going to be sent back home. Two days later a miracle happened; the immigration wrote his employers that they were prepared to extend his visa for another two years. We were so happy. The reason I was personally happy was because this is where his heart is and I just want him to be happy and to fulfil his dreams.

AA

Dear Pastor Matthew

I arrived in the UK 10 years ago and God gave me a word that He has given me an inheritance in this country. At the time I received the Word I was living in this country illegally, and to me it was like a dream that would never see the light of dawn.

I was unable to any sort of employment; even menial jobs were unavailable to me. I lived in constant fear and was very insecure. Lawyers were not interested in my case because they believed there was no substance to my case. My life seemed so worthless, I considered committing suicide.

It was not long before I received the news I dreaded most; my application to remain in the country was rejected. I was detained for three days and served a deportation order. However, God intervened and I was let off after two deportation attempts. This caused me to begin to pay attention to the Word of God.

God led me to KICC where I rededicated my life to God. I received spiritual support. I also obtained wisdom through Pastor Matthew's sermons and by studying the Word of God.

God has since worked many miracles in my life. In February, Pastor Matthew preached on the 24 hour miracle. During this time my British citizenship was approved. God's goodness to me has overwhelmed me.

Dear Pastor Matthew
The Lord has done great things in my life and in the life of my son.

I came to KICC as a divorced mother of one child. I was living in a council flat with rent arrears of over £5,000. I listened to the sermons of the Pastor and learnt how to wisely manage my resources. By divine intervention I was moved very quickly in to a flat under a regeneration scheme. I did not like the flat I was given. However, as I did not want to fall out of favour with the Council. I accepted the flat. I applied to buy the flat encouraged by the teachings I listened to at church.

The flat was valued at £105,000 and after the discount I was requested to pay £67,000. An estate agent recently valued the house at £150,000. A profit of £150%! I have learnt a lot from the teachings of Pastor Matthew. I am now looking for a second property so I can move out and rent my flat to tenants. The price of rent in my area is £1200 over month. Praise be to God Almighty!

My son had been given slips for bad behaviour by his school and the play centre. I was not pleased about this and continuously brought the matter before the Lord in prayer. Together we attended all the International Gathering of Champions Conference (IGOC) sessions. After the conference we spent time reading the Bible and praying together. When he returned to school his behaviour had improved greatly. One member of staff asked me what I had done to him! I no longer receive bad reports from the school and he is now in the top group for all the subjects at school. To God be the glory.